A Month of Miracles

Other New Hope Books by These Authors

Stronger Still: A Woman's Guide to Turning Your Hurt into Healing for Others
Edna Ellison

Deeper Still: A Woman's Study to a Closer Walk with God
Edna Ellison

Woman to Woman: Preparing Yourself to Mentor
Edna Ellison and Tricia Scribner

Journey to Confidence: Becoming Women Who Witness
Kimberly Sowell

"Friend to Friend" Series by Edna Ellison

Friend to Friend: Enriching Friendships Through a Shared Study of Philippians

Friendships of Faith: A Shared Study of Hebrews

Friendships of Purpose: A Shared Study of Ephesians

A MONTH *of* MIRACLES

30 STORIES *of* THE UNMISTAKABLE PRESENCE *of* GOD

WOMEN *by* DESIGN
EDNA ELLISON, KIMBERLY SOWELL, TRICIA SCRIBNER, MARIE ALSTON,
JOY BROWN, AND CHERIE NETTLES

NEW HOPE
PUBLISHERS
Birmingham, Alabama

New Hope® Publishers
P. O. Box 12065
Birmingham, AL 35202-2065
www.newhopepublishers.com

New Hope Publishers is a division of WMU®.

Library of Congress Cataloging-in-Publication Data
A month of miracles: 30 stories of the unmistakable presence of God / Women by Design.
    p. cm.
  ISBN 978-1-59669-209-1 (hc)
  1. Christian women--Religious life--Anecdotes. 2. Miracles--Anecdotes. 3. Presence of God--Anecdotes.
I. Women by Design (Organization)
BV4527.M623 2008
242--dc22

                        2007036092

ISBN-10: 1-59669-209-X
ISBN-13: 978-1-59669-209-1

N084135 • 0308 • 4.2M1

Dedication

Few people in this life lead others as Christ did, not with pomp and power, but as humble servants who gently direct and correct, encourage and guide. Edna Ellison has been that kind of leader to every member of the Women by Design team. More than six years ago, God took six women from very different walks of life to form Women by Design Ministries. Throughout that time, Edna has mentored every member in writing, and has been an encourager extraordinaire. When New Hope decided to publish *A Month of Miracles*, it seemed only fitting to dedicate this project to Edna Ellison, our precious friend and mentor, the matriarch of our team, who through tender love has guided us in a way that shows us exactly how Jesus would lead.

Edna, we love you!

Of course, each team member wants to say her own special, thank you:

To Edna—My sister endomorph! Thank you for loving to talk—especially to me, and thank you for allowing me to "jump on" and be your flea! I love you bunches! I think you're wonderful!—*Cherie*

To Edna Ellison, whose wisdom guides me, whose wit amuses me, whose "worrylessness" (lack of worry) amazes me, whose words (written and spoken) bless and inspire me. I love you, dear Edna!—*Joy*

Edna, you have the beautiful heart of a selfless servant. You have taught me so much about writing, and even more about walking with Jesus. Thank you for helping me grow in ministry for the Lord!—*Kimberly*

Edna, you are truly an inspiration, a woman after God's own heart. You are my spiritual mom in the Lord, and I love you dearly.—*Marie*

I prayed for 15 years for a mentor friend. If I had known it was going to be you, a friend beyond my dreams, I would have prayed with much more faith. Still, God in His mercy gave me far more than I knew to ask for (and yes, I know that preposition is dangling). You are my life mentor, my precious friend, and part of my family. I love you with all my heart.—*Tricia*

Table of Contents

INTRODUCTION 11

DAY 1: Miracle on 50th Street *by Joy Clary Brown*. 13
DAY 2: Just Dropping In *by Cherie Nettles* 17
DAY 3: When We Come to the End of Ourselves *by Tricia Scribner* 23
DAY 4: A Flaming Example *by Kimberly Sowell* 29
DAY 5: No Regrets! *by Marie Alston*. 33
DAY 6: The Miracle of Prayer *by Edna Ellison*. 37
DAY 7: Homecoming *by Tricia Scribner*. 41
DAY 8: The Rearview Mirror *by Cherie Nettles* 47
DAY 9: From a Far-Off Land *by Joy Clary Brown*. 53
DAY 10: The Miracle of the Lost Sheep *by Edna Ellison*. 57
DAY 11: The Three-for-One Special *by Kimberly Sowell*. 61
DAY 12: Ballerina Dreams *by Marie Alston* 65
DAY 13: We Win! *by Cherie Nettles* 69
DAY 14: At All Times and In All Times *by Joy Clary Brown* 75
DAY 15: Do You Have a Few Minutes? *by Edna Ellison* 79
DAY 16: A Change of Heart *by Kimberly Sowell* 85
DAY 17: Think Pink *by Kimberly Sowell* 89

DAY 18: In and Out of My Arms *by Kimberly Sowell* 95

DAY 19: A Sweet Gift of Love *by Joy Clary Brown* 99

DAY 20: Magnolia Miracle *by Edna Ellison* 103

DAY 21: Victory Scars *by Marie Alston* 107

DAY 22: Beautiful Feet *by Cherie Nettles* 111

DAY 23: A Simple Testimony *by Tricia Scribner* 115

DAY 24: The Blue Shepherd *by Edna Ellison* 119

DAY 25: God's Good Thoughts *by Tricia Scribner* .123

DAY 26: Eighty Dollars *by Marie Alston* 127

DAY 27: Not Just a Dream *by Tricia Scribner* 131

DAY 28: Christmas with Daddy *by Edna Ellison* 137

DAY 29: Making His Decision *by Joy Clary Brown* .143

DAY 30: When You Are Not the Miracle *by Cherie Nettles* 149

WOMEN *by* DESIGN, A MINISTRY 155

HOW TO USE THIS BOOK 157

Acknowledgments

More than six years ago, a group of women gathered to pray on the beach in South Carolina. They came from Maine, Louisiana, Alabama, California, South Carolina, and North Carolina. Each of these places made an impact on these Christians who dreamed of combining in a ministry called Women by Design. We are grateful for our varied backgrounds, our parents and other influences, and the unusual circumstances through which God gathered us to that pivotal point on the beach.

One dream birthed that day for Women by Design was *A Month of Miracles*, which would include 30 stories of "holy coincidences" God had allowed in our lives.

Today that dream has come true with the publication of this little book. Though it was a gift from God, it did not come easily. We gratefully thank many people for their help.

We are grateful to Andrea Mullins, publisher, New Hope Publishers, and her staff. Joyce Dinkins, managing editor, has given her guiding hands to this publication, blessing us in many ways as she has overseen the details. We thank the talented graphic designer, Sherry Hunt, for the beautiful pages. We thank the skilled copy editors, Jean Baswell, Ella Robinson, and Kathryne Solomon for their hard work.

We also owe our families, who have encouraged our work; and especially husbands who have filled in the gaps at home while we have written. Thank You, Almighty God, for allowing us to serve You and acknowledge Your presence in our lives.

Introduction

A Month *of* Miracles

By Women *by* Design Ministries
Six Ordinary Women Who See the Imprint of an Extraordinary God

As a ministry team, we six have prayed a long time about writing a book focusing on God's miraculous working in our lives. Every time we get together, we share something new and amazing He has done. Sometimes He has worked by suspending or supernaturally countering the natural order He has put in place. These events cannot be explained by any natural process, and we call them *miracles*. At other times, God has providentially orchestrated average circumstances in such a beyond-coincidence way that while these events may not be miracles in the strictest definition, they bear the unmistakable imprint of God's hand.

Regardless of what we call these "God events," we should remember two truths as we ponder their significance. First, miracles occur against the backdrop of stark human need, and we are right to thank God for these blessings in the midst of difficult, if not impossible, circumstances. Second, miracles serve an even greater purpose in God's magnificent plan. They authenticate the gospel message because they cannot be explained by man's reason and cause us to look for the Cause beyond us. God performs His mighty works so that we believe in Him and glorify Him. For this purpose, we share our stories, and we pray that through our witness you will believe in Him and be strengthened in your faith.

We have provided 30 stories, with discussion questions or meditations at the end of each, so that as an individual or as a group, you can celebrate His miraculous blessings as He strengths your faith.

A certain nobleman whose son was sick . . . implored [Jesus] to . . . heal his son, for he was at the point of death. Then Jesus said to him, "Unless you people see signs and wonders, you will by no means believe. . . . Go your way; your son lives." . . . And he himself believed, and his whole household. This again is the second sign Jesus did when He had come out of Judea into Galilee.

—John 4:46–54 (NKJV)

A Month of Miracles

———◆◆◆◆◆◆———

Miracle on 50th Street

By Joy Clary Brown

And my God will meet all your needs according to his glorious riches in Christ Jesus.
—Philippians 4:19 (NIV)

In all the world there is simply nothing like Christmas in New York! It's beautiful; it's wonderful; it's miraculous! You probably are familiar with the movie *Miracle on 34th Street*, but it might surprise you to learn that there was a lesser-known, yet no less significant, miracle on 50th Street.

It was Christmas 1986. Colored lights on street corners, in store windows, and in the eyes of children blinked like rhythmical dancing. Santas of every race, creed, and color were stationed beside red buckets as they jingled bells and collected money for the "less fortunate." Frigid air, slushy snow, roasted chestnuts, frantic shoppers, tired store clerks, and screeching traffic all harmonized like a maestro's symphony to make it what it was—Christmas in New York!

Our family had recently moved to New Jersey for my husband, Wayne, to serve as pastor of a mission church. The small congregation planned to go into New York City to see the *Christmas Spectacular* at Radio City Music Hall on 50th Street. Entenmann's Bakery and Maxwell House Coffee sponsored the show that year, and the combination of one bakery coupon and a coffee can lid from these sponsoring companies was worth a savings of five dollars per ticket for up to four tickets. Our church members had been saving bakery coupons and plastic coffee can lids for months.

With coupons and lids in hand, Wayne traveled to New York to purchase the tickets for our group. He patiently stood in a long ticket line, waiting his turn inside the magnificently decorated lobby of Radio City.

After purchasing the tickets, he was left with one extra coupon and coffee can lid. Turning to the person in line behind him, he saw a petite black lady with a pensive expression on her face. Offering her the coupon and coffee can lid, he inquired, "Would you like to have these? They will help you with your tickets."

When a stranger offers you *anything* in New York City, you are somewhat suspicious and reluctant to take it. She cautiously accepted his gift and moved up to the ticket window.

My husband maneuvered through the press of people and almost had reached the door leading to the sidewalk when the sound of a child's voice stopped him. "Mister, mister, will you please wait? My mama wants to talk to you." He turned to see a little girl about eight or nine years of age pushing through the crowd to stop him.

Wayne curiously stepped back inside the lobby when he noticed the same lady who had been in the ticket line behind him hurriedly trying to catch him. "Mister, I just want to thank you," she panted.

Wayne replied, "Oh, you're welcome."

With a serious tone in her voice she repeated, "No, mister, I *really* want to thank you. You see, coming to this show is the only thing my baby wanted for Christmas. While I was standing in the line behind you, I read the prices and realized that we did not have enough money to buy the tickets. I prayed, *Dear God, this is all my baby wants for Christmas and I can't give it to her. Would You please provide a way for her to see this show?* Right after that, sir, you turned and handed me those things. I didn't know what they were, but when I gave them to the lady at the window, she told me they were worth five dollars per ticket . . . ten dollars!"

With shaky hands she showed Wayne a small amount of money she had left in her palm. "Look, mister, now I can even buy my baby a hamburger before the show begins."

The three of them—my husband, a stranger, and her "baby"—stood in the bustling lobby of Radio City Music Hall joining hands in prayer and thanking God.

Upon returning home, Wayne bounded through our front door and shouted, "Joy, Meri Beth, Molly, come here. Have I got a story for you!"

The four of us sat on the couch and cried as Wayne related the events of that afternoon. Through tears I choked out the words, "Isn't that just like God? Before the lady even knew she had the *need*, He had already provided the *answer*!"

Thus it has been, and thus it will always be. Our loving God knows what we need long before we do. And He already has provided the answer to our every need on another Christmas 2,000 years ago.

◆◆◆ MEDITATION MOMENTS ◆◆◆

1. What do you think is the most pressing need in your life right now?

2. Cultivate the habit of quoting Philippians 4:19 each time you are tempted to worry about that need.

Just Dropping In

BY CHERIE NETTLES

"Every place that the sole of your foot will tread upon, I have given you."
—Joshua 1:3 (NKJV)

M-I-R-C-L-E.
"Nice try. Now try again. Sound it out: MIR-A-CLE."
"M-I-R-A-C-L-E—miracle!"
"Good girl; that's right!"

I'll never forget when my daughter Ashleigh was in second grade, and the bonus word on her spelling list was *miracle*. What a big word for such a little girl. We practiced spelling the word all week, and finally on the night before her test, she got it.

Ashleigh beamed at the accomplishment, but then held a look of dismay.

"Mommy, what is a miracle?" I told her a miracle was something that only God could do, like healing a sick person or making a baby in a mommy's tummy or something else really big! As Ashleigh processed the definition, I expected a zillion questions to follow, but instead Ashleigh began to write sentences with her spelling words.

"Mommy, do you want to hear my sentence for *miracle*?" I smiled. Her face lit up as she read, "Miracle—I am a miracle." I laughed through tears (the greatest emotion) and told her she was a precious miracle, but I wondered if she would really understand how God had already worked a miracle in her life.

When Ashleigh was 2 years old, my husband, Mike, and I took her and her brother Alex, then 5, to Myrtle Beach, South Carolina. We read advertisements all week about the children's play area at a local water park and knew this would be a great escape from all of the beach sand Ashleigh had eaten or collected in her swim diaper.

It was an especially hot day as Mike chatted with the family behind us in the admission line. The family shared how they traveled from Ohio every year to vacation in Myrtle Beach. This year things were different for them because they had a new family member, their 13-year-old nephew. In the past year he had lost his mother. Then his grandmother who had custody of him died unexpectedly, leaving this family as the only ones to care for him. So, with only two weeks' notice, they had a new addition, who had traveled with them on vacation. The relationship had felt strained for them, since they never before had spent any time with the boy.

My husband smiled at him and patted his shoulder, telling him he was in for a fun day. The mother further explained how he really wasn't supposed to be on the trip, but because of unexplained legal circumstances, he was able to join them much earlier than anticipated. The boy looked up and gave a slight grin at Mike.

We spent much of our afternoon sitting around baby pools. After rallying confidence, Alex headed to his first waterslide. We followed him to the "big boy" slide, which stood a little over five feet. We waved him on, wading in the water below to catch our brave boy. Ashleigh clung to her daddy's leg, repeating, "It not my turn; it not my turn." We were confident she wouldn't be sliding on this trip.

As Alex continued up and down the slide, Mike suddenly looked at me and said, "Where's Ashleigh?" My heart sank.

Alex yelled, "Ashleigh, get down!" I looked up as Ashleigh's little feet reached the final step at the top of the slide. Mike ran to get her, but running in water made him move at a slug's pace. When Ashleigh stood up on the platform, she began to scream. Realizing how frightened she was, the three of us yelled, "Stand still, Ashleigh. Daddy's coming!"

As soon as Mike reached the water's edge, our fears became reality: Ashleigh slipped on the watery platform and began plummeting headfirst toward the concrete sidewalk. I screamed and fell to my knees. I cried out for someone to help her, knowing she would break her neck in the fall. No one was in sight. Mike reached the slide's edge, but not in time to catch her. At that very moment, arms from nowhere stretched out and caught Ashleigh, as I heard someone say, "You're OK, little girl. Here's your daddy."

We looked up in astonishment. Retrieving Ashleigh, Mike realized it was the boy that had lost his family and had nowhere else to go, the boy that was not supposed to be on this vacation, the 13-year-old who was standing near the baby pool instead of careening down the big slides with his new family—that boy!

Today I know why he arrived earlier than scheduled. I know why he got tired of sliding and walked off from his group, and why his new family vacationed in South Carolina. God orchestrated the soles of his feet that particular day, and he was a vessel God used to perform a miracle. He saved our daughter's life. Their "chance" meeting was this day.

In tears, Mike began to thank the boy. (I was a basket case, sobbing spread-eagle in the baby pool.) Mike told him that God had brought him to Myrtle Beach to save our daughter's life, and that even though it may not have been the way he wanted to come, he was there for a miraculous purpose. The boy said, "Yeah, I guess I am. I'm glad I was here today."

Just like Ashleigh, you, too, are a miracle. You may not have felt it lately, but God has orchestrated your steps that you might trust Him with your life. Today, you may not be walking your pathway of choice, but keep looking, because a miracle may just "drop" your way!

ᐧᐧᐧ᙮ MEDITATION MOMENTS ᙮ᐧᐧᐧ

1. Do you feel as though the soles of your feet need direction? If so, write Proverbs 3:5–6 on an index card. Keep it with you until you hide it in your heart and trust it in your soul, because the Lord will direct your soles' path.

2. Like the 13-year-old boy, have you ever felt out of place in a new or confusing situation?

3. How did God change an awkward time in your life into a good or a new opportunity?

————◆◆◆◆◆◆◆◆————

When We Come to the End of Ourselves

By Tricia Scribner

"Not by might nor by power, but by My Spirit," says the Lord *of hosts.*
—Zechariah 4:6 (NKJV)

The darkened delivery room of a small Baptist hospital in Zimbabwe, Africa, was quiet, except for the occasional clicking on and off of my flashlight. Miri, a newborn with a disorder known as meconium aspiration pneumonia, lay in a nearby incubator. Between snatches of fitful sleep, I used my flashlight to monitor her struggle from my vantage point on a nearby delivery room bed. Each time I switched on the flashlight I wondered if she would still be breathing.

At moments like these, I seriously questioned why I had come to Africa a second time to volunteer for a month as a missionary nurse. The truth was, I believed God had called me. Also, I had returned this time with a career missionary nurse-midwife friend, Pam, providing a great learning opportunity for me. I would work in labor and delivery with her in a 100-bed hospital that boasted 150–200 deliveries a month, often without the benefit of a physician.

The first work week brought one crisis after another. The missionary laboratory technologists had gone home on stateside assignment, as had the missionary doctor. Ultrasound equipment was nonexistent, the x-ray machine was down, and we were short on even basic medicines. The ambulance was wrecked, the phones were often out of order, and the roads to the next nearest hospital were frequently washed out by seasonal rains. Of gargantuan importance in my own mind was the fact that we had no physician. With the missionary doctor gone, the government only sporadically sent physicians to the hospital to help. The perpetual lack of supplies and personnel thwarted our efforts at every turn, and even minor complications escalated into life-threatening situations.

By the end of those first few trying days, I was exhausted and angry—angry I didn't know more, that there weren't enough medicines, that we couldn't save more babies and mothers, and most of all, angry at God, who seemed to have dropped me off in some obscure African outpost and left for more important endeavors. Death had an unfair advantage in this place. It came almost nonchalantly, as though it belonged.

Then Miri was born. The delivery was progressing normally when we noted the signs of fetal distress. A day after birth she couldn't suck to take nourishment, she had fluid in her lungs, and her skin had taken on a bluish hue. Pam opened the medicine cabinet to choose from the paltry supply. The baby needed intravenous fluids and antibiotics to survive. Pam strapped the baby's head to the table to prevent injury as we searched for a scalp vein. After several failed attempts, she settled for a hand vein and we prayed it would stay open long enough to give the needed fluids and medication.

After placing Miri in the incubator, I talked with her mom. Miri's parents had waited four long years for her. My heart ached for them. In America, Miri's illness was manageable, but here she would likely die.

So there I lay that night, flashlight in hand to monitor her breathing; having no pediatric IV monitoring equipment, I watched to assure the 1,000-milliliter bag of intravenous fluid ran at a miniscule four drops per minute.

Between flashlight checks, doubts plagued me. Did God care what was happening here? If Miri died, was God still good? I was afraid—afraid that if she died, I wouldn't have the courage to return to work the next day, or any day after.

I prayed, *Lord, I know by all logic, this child should die. We don't have the medicines or the equipment to save her. We have done everything we know to do, and it is not enough. Lord, we need to know You are here. Please, don't let her die.*

I desperately wanted to be able to pray that God's will be done, no matter what, but that was easier when I was fairly sure things would turn out the way I wanted. It was harder when I had to decide if God was still all He claimed to be if the miracle didn't come—if we failed—if Miri died.

The next day, a doctor arrived at the hospital and examined Miri, making treatment recommendations. As a friend of Pam's, whom she trusted, the doctor bolstered our sagging spirits and reminded us God was at work.

Still, the days wore on; the doctor left; and we waited. At times, Miri seemed to rally. But two weeks later, as I left for the US, her prognosis was still uncertain. Once home,

I involved myself in the familiar daily routine, but my mind often wandered back to Africa and Miri. What would God's final word be?

Finally, a letter arrived to tell me the news I had waited so long to hear: Miri had gotten well and was sent home with her parents. I learned that day that because God is good, He often waits with anticipation to give the long-awaited miracle, but He does wait: He waits for pride to give way to humility, for knowledge to defer to wisdom, and for anxiety to burn itself out into abiding hope.

And perhaps the miracle isn't the greatest work God did among us. The truth is, Miri would have enjoyed heaven more than earth, and God would have been able to reveal Himself to Miri's parents through loss and sorrow if He had permitted her to die. Still, this time He chose for her to live. He knew we needed to grow in character traits that reflected a deepening trust in Him. This kind of faith, when mature, holds firm in the most difficult circumstance. It is the kind of faith He stands ready to give, but only when we come to the end of ourselves.

1. How strong is your faith when the prayed-for miracle doesn't come?

2. How has God strengthened your faith by delaying an answer to your prayers?

A Flaming Example

By Kimberly Sowell

And we know that all things work together for good to those who love God,
to those who are the called according to His purpose.
—Romans 8:28 (NKJV)

"OK, Mom, we'll go tomorrow instead. That's fine. See you then." Click. Whenever I invite my mother to go shopping for the day, she always says yes, but on this particular occasion she said no. Mom was making doll clothes for my niece, and she wanted to finish up the sewing project before taking off with me for a day of bargain hunting.

Oh well, I thought. *At least I can look forward to visiting my sister and her family tonight.* I moped into the bathroom to fix my hair. What a flop! I hadn't had such a bad hair day in a very long time. *This is not shaping up to be a good day*, I thought.

The morning passed slowly. Finally lunchtime came and went, and I got my daughter Julia down for her nap. At last! I had an hour to get ready before leaving to visit my sister, but I really wanted to go upstairs to my office first to check my email. *Well*, I thought, *I should try to do something with this hair first. I look awful!*

As I walked into the bathroom, the smell of smoke lay heavily in the air. My panic level was rising with every whiff, but I managed to keep my composure. *Is it my curling iron? Hair dryer? Hot rollers? No. Something in the bathtub? No. Maybe the smoke is coming inside from a fire in the backyard. No, nothing was burning in the yard. What else could it be?* As I turned my head to look for the phone, I saw rings of smoke rising from my decorative bath towels. Upon closer examination, I found a fist-sized hole that had burned in one towel, and the ring around the hole was lit up with orange cinders. The smoke and cinders told me the towel was just about to burst into flames. I quickly threw the towel in the sink and doused it with water from the faucet. Crisis over.

I quickly surmised that my house had nearly burned down from the most unusual of circumstances. Intense winter sunbeams bore through my bathroom window, reflected off a brass mirror resting on the bathroom counter, converging on a singular point on the towel. A moment later, and the bathroom would have been in flames.

After the adrenaline ceased pumping through my veins, I began to realize what God had done for me that day. Had I gone shopping with my mother, I would not have been at home, and the house would have burned down. *Thank You, God, for having a greater purpose for life's little disappointments.* Had my hair turned out when I fixed it that morning, I wouldn't have gone into the bathroom to catch the towel before it burst into flames. *Thank You, God, for having a greater purpose in how my hair looks.* Had I first gone upstairs to check my email, I would have come back downstairs to find smoke and flames. *Thank You, God, for helping me prioritize even the most insignificant affairs of life.*

I reflected on what had happened for days after the almost fire. Why did God let the towel burn in the first place? If He hadn't intended to permit the house to catch on fire, why let the towel smolder and allow such a close call? Then I realized the great value in God's intentions. God does everything with purpose, and He was teaching me a lesson. God has said, "Look with your eyes and hear with your ears, and fix your mind on everything I show you; for you were brought here so that I might show them to you" (Ezekiel 40:4 NKJV). Through this near-tragic experience, I was reminded of the many wonderful ways of God:

- God has supreme knowledge of my past, present, and future: "You know my sitting down and my rising up; You understand my thought afar off" (Psalm 139:2 NKJV).
- I am constantly under the care of God: "The LORD has been mindful of us; He will bless us" (Psalm 115:12 NKJV).
- God gives attention to every detail in my life: "A man's heart plans his way, but the LORD directs his steps" (Proverbs 16:9 NKJV).
- God works all details (regardless of whether they seem positive or negative to me) for my good: "And we know that all things work together for good to

those who love God, to those who are the called according to His purpose" (Romans 8:28 NKJV).

Value of Replacing a smoldered bath towel: $12.99.
Value of Being reminded of God's sovereignty: priceless.

⤙•••• MEDITATION MOMENTS ••••⤚

1. Have you complained lately about a circumstance in your life? Are you disappointed about something that didn't go as you had hoped? Read Psalm 115:12*a* again. Thank God for His mindfulness of you.

2. Romans 8:28 reminds us that God is always at work, blessing us as a part of His greater purpose for our lives. As you reflect on God's blessings, are you fulfilling God's purpose for your life?

Day 5

No Regrets!

By Marie Alston

To everything there is a season, a time for every purpose under heaven.
—Ecclesiastes 3:1–2 (NKJV)

As I walked down the aisle holding on to my father's arm, I could see my husband-to-be standing at the altar. Mr. Tall, Dark, and Handsome, Charles Emanuel Alston. He was stunning with his sleek physique in his white tuxedo. It was hard to believe I was actually getting married.

When I was growing up, it was said if you weren't married by age 18, or at least after you had finished high school, you were doomed to be an old maid. I finished high school and college without being married and accepted my lot in life. According to my mother, I was going to stay an old maid because I was too opinionated and picky. I told my mom I wasn't settling for just "any old thing." I was a product of the 70s era; the man I married had to love the Lord, and have a J-O-B—job! And, of course, being tall, dark, and handsome wouldn't hurt either. My generation of women wanted to be independent, liberated, and accepted for our minds; yet we still wanted men to hold the door for us and, if the occasion arose, give up their seats for us.

I had received my education, and I felt I had to use my degree before settling down into marriage. I also wanted to make some money and have the privilege of learning how to manage it to pay back my student loans. I didn't want to enter marriage in debt. If and when I accomplished all these things, *then* I would be ready to settle down and get married.

Charles and I dated off and on in high school and some also while I was in college, but no serious sparks were flying for me, though he proposed to me right after high school and college. He went on with his life, dating other people, and I went on with mine.

Finally, I got a job teaching. I think Mother had almost given up on the idea of my ever getting married and providing her with more grandchildren. I had taught school for more than four years, when Prince Charming came along again. This time there seemed to be a different aura about him. He seemed more confident, and we talked more about the Lord and what He had been doing in our lives. I began to look at him differently. We dated for a while, and, yes, he had a job! After five months of dating, he popped the big question; I said yes; and the rest is history.

I was 26 years old and Charles was 29 when we spoke our vows. I have no regrets about waiting for Mr. Right. It was one of the happiest days of my life.

It was a beautiful, warm, though wintry, day in December. We stood before that altar and pledged life and love to one another "for better for worse, for richer for poorer, in sickness and in health, till death us do part, so help me God," believing in our hearts that we would grow old and gray together. Little did I know that day, those vows would become my sustaining grace in the years to come.

When we first spoke our vows, we didn't fully comprehend the significance of our words. Charles and I lived together through some very tough "for better or for worse" and "for richer for poorer" days. Some days we were poorer than others, but we made it through by holding onto God's unchanging hand.

"Till death do us part" came for me on March 15, 2005. I awoke to find my beloved gasping for breath. I didn't know those gasping sounds were his last breaths, but God called him home—congestive heart failure at 53. I never thought on December 20, 1980, when I walked down that aisle and took those vows, that fewer than 25 years later I would be a young widow left to raise four children alone.

Do I have any regrets? Do I regret going to college instead of accepting Charles's marriage proposal after high school? Then maybe we would have had more days together. No regrets! Do I regret not accepting his marriage proposal after graduating from college? No regrets. God had a plan and a purpose for my life, nurturing me during those single years, preparing me spiritually and mentally to be a wife, mother, friend, and helpmate.

Do I regret waiting on the Lord to bring Mr. Right back into my life after a period of time? No regrets, because there is a time and a season for everything; Charles had some sowing and growing up in the Lord to do as well.

After waiting on the Lord to do a work in us, He brought us back together.

We lived a full life, serving Him with gladness, coming before His presence with singing. We ministered, sang, and laughed a lot in the Lord, so when God sent the death angel—there were no regrets.

My greatest testimony to God's grace is that I sang a song as we left the emergency room the morning Charles died. He and I had spent our lives together, sharing the gospel of Jesus Christ, and the goal, the prize, was to get to heaven. Charles is already home. One day I will join him. Amen, and amen!

——•◆•◆• MEDITATION MOMENTS •◆•◆•——

1. Will you have regrets when death knocks at your door? Maybe you've already lost a loved one and you don't know how to go on with your own life with the regrets that haunt you. Release those regrets to Jesus; He is more than able to sustain you.

2. When was the last time you sang praise to God for the assurance of an eternal home in heaven for those who have Jesus as their Savior? Reflect on the glorious moment you will meet your Savior face-to-face.

A Month of Miracles

————◆◆◆◆◆◆◆◆◆————

The Miracle of Prayer

BY EDNA ELLISON

The prayer of a righteous man is powerful and effective.
—James 5:16 (NIV)

When I became a Christian, God truly performed a miracle in my life. I had been a mean little girl who had faced her sin for the first time. My heart was changed after I asked Him for forgiveness and promised to live every day with Him in my heart, to lead me in everything I do. I drifted off to sleep that night after making everything right with Almighty God and accepting His peace. When I woke up the next morning, the world had changed: the flowers seemed brighter; the sky seemed bluer; and the birds sang sweeter in every tree. I still remember the song in my heart and the deep-down joy of being a new Christian. I had truly experienced what I had heard about from other Christians: the miracle of being born again.

It was time for my baby sister, Phyllis, to be born, and my father took Mother to the hospital. The doctor said she was not ready to have the baby, and so we started home. While my father got out to buy a few needed items at a local vegetable market on our town's Main Street, I walked along the sidewalk and watched a little boy with an ice-cream cone. He sat on a low wall near the drugstore next door, with his legs swinging happily as they dangled off the side. He grinned as he licked the ice cream, which was melting fast. His dark skin shone as the vanilla ice cream glistened on his lips and cheeks. How I longed for the cool, sweet taste! He smiled at everyone who passed by. Then I saw a sign over the drugstore door:

> ## Special Sale
> ### Ice-Cream Cones
> ### 5¢

Wow! I thought. *What an unbelievable sale!* I wanted an ice cream really badly as I sweated in the blistering heat. Mother was in the car talking to my younger brother, Jim, and my father was too busy in the outdoor market to give me a nickel, and he probably didn't have one to spare, I figured.

As the sun beat down on that July day, I thought, *I'd love ice cream to cool me off. . . .* And then I thought of the perfect idea: *I'm a Christian now. I'll pray with power—not as a skinny, weak little girl anymore, but with the power of a Christian.*

Then God will answer. I walked away from the boy with the ice cream, moved closer to the drugstore corner, bowed my head, and closed my eyes, with people passing. *Lord,* I said, *I want a nickel for an ice-cream cone. A nickel, a nickel, a nickel—or five pennies—however You want to do it. I just want a nickel for an ice-cream cone.*

When I opened my eyes, to my surprise, a nickel lay between my toes. I was amazed. Had it been there all along? Did a kind passerby see a little girl praying and place it there on the sidewalk while my eyes were closed? Did God hear my prayer and instantly respond by zapping a nickel out of nowhere to land on the sidewalk just between my toes where I could see it? I couldn't figure it out. I only know that God instantly answered my prayer!

I've often wondered why God answered such a selfish prayer from a little girl. I believe it was to teach me the power of prayer. From that miraculous moment, I've been convinced God answers prayers. I once prayed for a new Bible, and an aunt gave me hers. I also prayed for a better job for my father, and he got it! When I grew up and started dating, I prayed for one certain young man to show me attention, and he asked me to marry him! I prayed often over our children when they were sick with fever, and the fever went down. I once prayed for God to help me find an expensive watch belonging to my husband, and we quickly found it under a pile of socks in a dresser drawer. The first time I prayed for his healing when he had a severe toothache in the middle of the night, God took the pain away instantly and he went immediately to sleep. However, I know the power of prayer is not an exercise in instant gratification. When I pray, the most important thing God changes is *me*. As we mature in prayer, we learn to bend to His will and pray according to His desire, not ours.

I no longer pray, *Lord, I want a nickel*. But I do pray for financial needs. I no longer pray for instant answers to my prayer because I've learned He answers in His timing, not mine. I no longer pray for "yes" answers because I realize that, like a child, I sometimes ask for ice cream when God knows I need vegetables for my own good. I know that He has to say no for my benefit and my spiritual growth at times, and at other times He tells me to wait and learn patience from Him. However, I'll never forget that first wonderful, miraculous prayer when God provided a simple little coin, a nickel, just to show me His power and love on day one of my walk of a lifetime with Him.

⸺⸰⸰⸰ MEDITATION MOMENTS ⸰⸰⸰⸺

1. Have you ever experienced a miraculous event that can't be explained in human terms?

2. How has God been faithful as He has responded to your prayers? How would you tell a younger person how to pray?

Homecoming

BY TRICIA SCRIBNER

I will remember the deeds of the LORD; *yes, I will remember your miracles of long ago.*
I will meditate on all your works and consider all your mighty deeds.
—Psalm 77:11–12 (NIV)

Randy, my husband, and I traveled to Mexico on one of our first volunteer missions trips in the summer of 1980. Our small team consisted of Christians from various churches who combined efforts and skills to provide medical care in impoverished areas of Mexico. Near the end of the trip, we arrived at an orphanage, where we held a medical clinic for the community. As a public health nurse, I was assigned the task of examining about 30 orphans who lived there.

They lined up around the room, backs against the walls. One by one I listened to hearts and looked in ears. About two-thirds of the way around the room, I came across a three-year-old girl with brassy hair from malnutrition and an impish smile. Her thumb was firmly wedged into her mouth. *"Como se llama?"* I asked in a feeble attempt at Spanish. "Neli," she said. I began to cry. *Of course*, I thought, *anyone would weep, looking across this room of little ones who longed for mommies to hold them.* Still, I couldn't explain why I wept while examining this particular child. Through tears, I wrote on the top of her examination card, "I want this little girl for my child."

Our time together was brief. I finished examining her and went on to check the rest of the children, still fighting back tears. What had come over me? Randy and I had been married for nine years—nine years without children—by choice. We had no reason to suspect we couldn't have biological children and no desire to adopt. But once I returned home, the image of the little girl stuck in my mind. Finally, I talked with Randy. Could we consider trying to adopt her? He said he didn't feel strongly about it, but if I did choose to pursue adoption, I would have to do the footwork.

I began calling US lawyers, social service and adoption agencies, and governmental departments, searching for someone who could help us with the adoption. "You have to get a lawyer in Mexico," I was told repeatedly. After several dead ends, I finally found a lawyer in Mexico who would process the papers.

After months of verbal conversations, completing and returning papers to the lawyer, and getting physical exams, blood work, a social services home study, and psychological evaluations, we had fulfilled all the requirements. The adoption, we were told, was final.

A Month of Miracles

Even though Neli was legally our child, we still hadn't gotten her visa to enter the US, so she remained in Mexico. In the meantime, the lawyer said the adoption papers were ready for us to pick up, which would require a trip to Mexico. We would not get to see Neli. The orphanage director would pick up the papers from the lawyer and would meet us at a hotel. When we arrived, her somber countenance told us the news was bad. The lawyer had agreed to let her give us the completed paperwork on the condition that we must pay more money. All the months of agony, praying, and dreaming of our child were going up in smoke in an instant.

Finally, we agreed to pay an amount we thought reasonable, recognizing that the complexity of the work may have justified additional charges. Reluctantly, the orphanage director gave us the signed papers and we returned home.

With papers in hand, only the visa stood between us and our child; at least that's what we thought. Then we received a call from the orphanage director, saying government officials had come to visit. They were questioning the legality of Neli's adoption and had suggested a long-lost relative in Mexico wanted to adopt her. The director explained to them that Neli's adoption was already final. We would later learn of a stigma associated with Mexican children being adopted by US families, though we had done everything legally.

With tensions high, Neli was moved to a safe location to await the visa's arriving and our coming to get her. The days were agonizingly long. We could do nothing to change the situation, or to fully understand it, for that matter. When my anxiety threatened to spiral out of control, Randy offered assurance: "If God wants us to have this child, even two governments can't stop it; she will be our child."

Almost a year after we had first met Neli, the visa did come through, and we traveled to Mexico to bring our child, now nearly five years old, home. After all we had endured, I feared arriving at the border, only to hear them say she could not come home with us. My fears were not justified. We passed through the border without problems, and immediately drove to the nearby Iron Skillet restaurant, where we called home to friends and family. "We've crossed the border. We're bringing her home!" The whoops and hollers of joy on the other end of the line buoyed us up for the 15-hour drive home. The following morning we arrived home at 5:30 A.M. to almost 30 relatives—grandmom, aunts, uncles, and cousins—deluging us with hugs.

When it was all said and done, more than 50 government and other agency officials in two countries had helped us, including immigration and consulate officials, lawyers, doctors, social agencies, pastors, and psychologists. Above it all, God calmly went about His business, orchestrating His perfect plan. Neli is now 27 years old. Looking back, our yearlong ordeal seems but a blip on the time-line of life, reminding me to trust God, who alone sees the end from the very beginning.

━━•••• MEDITATION MOMENTS ••••━━

1. In hindsight, what events in your life reveal that God was at work, though you couldn't see it at the time?

2. How does God's past faithfulness influence your attitude in a current difficult situation?

———◆◆◆◆◆◆◆———

The Rearview Mirror

BY CHERIE NETTLES

"When you pass through the waters, I will be with you;
and when you pass through the rivers, they will not sweep over you."
—Isaiah 43:2 (NIV)

Mike, pull over! I'm scared to death!"

Mike calmly said, "Cherie, calm down. Everything will be OK."

The rain pelted our car in sheets. Lightning snapped overhead while thunder roared in our ears as we traveled down I-95 to my husband's grandmother's house in St. George, South Carolina. As my voice grew louder, the children raised their voices in a duel of "John Jacob Jinglehimer-Schmidt." When Alex, our son, reached his highest tone to "*da-da-duh-da-da-duh-da-da*," I raised my voice to a louder level, and that was all Mike could take. He said, "Cherie, calm down. You're going to upset the children."

The wind blew, causing our car to swerve, and I screamed again, "Mike, pull over!" He leaned closer to me and said, "Why don't we pray?"

After a very long prayer, the rain subsided. My husband looked in the rearview mirror and said, "Cherie, look behind you. I want you to see what we have come through." Then he added, "In order to get out of a storm, you must go through it."

I find that life is like that thunderstorm. In order to get through the stormy trials of life, we must walk through them and not stop in the middle. On the other side is where we find the sunshine. As Christians, we may not know what the future holds, but we know who holds the future.

Scripture says, "When you pass through the waters, I will be with you; and when you pass through the rivers, they will not sweep over you" (Isaiah 43:2 NIV). Not only do I believe this word of God in my heart, I also have walked through the deep waters that I felt would sweep over me. God was faithful to His word, and as I continued to walk, He brought me through the trial.

On October 19, 2002, I woke up to an unusual pressure on my right side. I scheduled a doctor's appointment and my gynecologist said I had a benign (noncancerous) tumor on my uterus. He told me it was not serious but would cause a little inconvenience, because it would have to be surgically removed. The doctor also drew blood for a CA-125 test, which is an ovarian tumor indicator. It came back elevated. During the next week, I had four more tests run that landed me in an oncologist's office. (An oncologist is a cancer doctor.) I was 40 years old, a wife, a mother, and now an ovarian cancer patient? I began to question God. Would He allow me to have cancer? I was devastated! I begged God for a word, and He tenderly replied, *Cherie, be still and know that I am God.* My friend, that was not the word I was looking for!

I had surgery in late October, and my worst fears became a reality. Before the surgery, my doctors felt certain I did not have cancer; however, when the doctor told Mike his findings from the surgery, the surgical biopsies revealed something different. I had stage 3C ovarian cancer that had spread throughout my pelvic area and into my stomach, and chemotherapy was needed.'

I continued to cry out, begging God for a word. He continued, *Be still and know that I am God.* Each night I cried out the words to the Rich Mullins song, "Hold Me Jesus." I would repeatedly sing, *"Hold me Jesus, 'cause I'm shaking like a leaf; You have been King of my glory; Won't You be my Prince of Peace."* And in that room I did find His peace.

November 5 arrived, and as usual, my husband spent the day with me in the hospital. Mike prayed over me as I slept, because he had seen the hopelessness in my eyes. After he left that evening, he called me at about 11:00 P.M. I could tell he was elated. "Cherie, I've found your word from God. It's Psalm 86. Read it; read it right now!" I hung up and began reading Psalm 86. I drifted off to sleep. At 4:00 A.M. on November 6, I awoke to the most beautiful still, quiet voice. You know that voice—the voice of God. God said, *Cherie, be confident in Me and be at peace for there is no more cancer.* Now that's a word! I reveled in the moment, wondering if I was dreaming. God then prompted me to journal what He had told me. I pulled my journal to my side and wrote, *"At 4:00 A.M. God woke me up and told me there was no more cancer."* I drifted back to sleep.

At 6:00 A.M., my doctor flung open the door and said, "Cherie, I have good news for you!" He had sent my lab reports to another pathology hospital and gotten the report back the previous evening. The report concluded that my tumor was cancerous but noninvasive. That meant it couldn't spread! We both knew what he had seen during surgery was different from what he was telling me now. Then the doctor added that since it could not spread, I was cured and didn't need chemotherapy. I told him I already knew, and asked if I could read my journal to him. He smiled, and I shared what God had prompted me to write. The doctor reached over and wrapped his arms around me, kissed me on the cheek, and said, "My child, God has smiled upon you!"

Mike was right; once again, God was faithful. This I could see through my "rearview mirror." As I looked behind me, I saw the storm I'd been through, and the view ahead was the sunshine awaiting me on the other side.

A Month of Miracles

━◆◆ MEDITATION MOMENTS ◆◆━

1. What has been your most difficult life circumstance?

2. What is your perspective from the "rearview mirror" of this circumstance? How does looking back help you grow spiritually?

From a Far-Off Land

BY JOY CLARY BROWN

From the east I summon a bird of prey; from a far-off land, a man to fulfill my purpose.
What I have said, that will I bring about; what I have planned, that will I do.
—Isaiah 46:11 (NIV)

Just before they were to leave, I got a call from Vicki. I could tell by her voice she was concerned about something.

"Joy," she said. "Please pray. The eyeglasses we were supposed to take for the medical clinic have been stopped at customs. For some unknown reason, the authorities will not let them get through unless we pay a huge amount for shipping. This has never happened before and those in charge of the ministry don't feel it would be a wise use of ministry monies to pay such a high fee. Please pray for a miracle."

The entire two weeks they were gone, I prayed consistently about the eye-glasses. I could hardly wait to hear how God miraculously allowed them through customs and how everything was fine. However, I was not prepared for the report of what really happened. When Vicki returned home, through tears and much emotion, she related the following story.

They were not able to take the glasses. The authorities were unrelenting about the high fee they were charging to allow the glasses through customs. Boxes of eyeglasses had to be left stateside. Meanwhile, in the Ukraine, the ministries in the orphanages, prisons, churches, and medical clinics went well. The team sensed God's presence in all they did.

One day, a lady from Sweden unexpectedly arrived at the medical clinic. She explained that she had heard often of the work of Dr. Krupin, the Ukrainian physician who operates the clinic with few supplies and almost no salary. She had brought something with her she wanted to donate if it would be of use to the clinic. The workers followed her to her car. They could hardly believe their eyes. This precious Swedish lady had brought boxes of eyeglasses!

The two weeks of missions work came to an end. The medical clinic, housed in a church, was concluding. The final patient was waiting in line. When he stepped forward, the missionary doctor immediately recognized he was suffering from an advanced eye disease, which resulted in extreme vision loss. This patient needed to be fitted with a strong prescription of glasses, but where could they go to find the specific kind of glasses he needed?

Suddenly the doctor remembered something he had seen in a box given by the Swedish lady. It was a pair of glasses he had put to the side, because they were so strong the average person could not use them. He hurriedly brought the glasses and placed them on the nearly blind patient. The man began rejoicing and praising God. He could see once again!

I had been praying for a miracle that the eyeglasses could make it through customs. God had a different and a better plan. He summoned someone from *a far-off land* to *fulfill His purpose*. The boxes of glasses stuck at customs did not have the kind of glasses that could help the man; the ones from Sweden did.

God's love is so personal; He goes to any length to meet our needs. The last patient on the last day of the medical clinic experienced God's love firsthand.

What happened to all the glasses left at customs? The next group traveling to the Ukraine took them without even a hint of trouble. God says, "What I have planned, that will I do" (Isaiah 46:11 NIV).

⸺•⸰• Meditation Moments •⸰•⸺

1. Have you ever had a specific need met by a total stranger, as in the case of the visually impaired man and the lady from Sweden?

2. In Isaiah 46:11, God assures that what He has planned, He will do. Read Jeremiah 29:11 to see what God has planned for you. Thank Him for His goodness.

—◆—◆◆◆◆◆◆◆◆◆—◆—

The Miracle of the Lost Sheep

BY EDNA ELLISON

"Rejoice with me; I have found my lost sheep."
—Luke 15:6 (NIV)

When my children were two and five, we lived on Caldwell Street in Clinton, South Carolina. Two blocks away in one direction was a large highway, with traffic that we could hear occasionally, rumbling down a nearby hill. Two blocks in the other direction was a nice home where our pastor and his family lived, and one block past his house was our wonderful church, which we loved.

One night we were awakened by the telephone at 2:30 A.M. Our pastor's wife said to my sleepy husband, "Snow, this is Laura—Reverend Floyd Hellams's wife. Jack is here."

I watched as my husband shook his head and moved the receiver to his other ear. "What?"

"Jack is here. Your son, Jack, is here."

Snow jumped out of bed and ran across the hall where he found our son's empty bed. "I'll be right there."

I asked what was going on, and he explained that Jack was missing from his bed, and that he was in the Hellamses' home. He didn't understand, but he was going to get Jack and find out the story behind these bewildering facts. I was to stay at home with Patsy. He'd be back shortly.

When he returned, he explained.

Mrs. Hellams had awakened in the night thinking she heard one of her children call, "Mama." She got up and checked each of their bedrooms, but all three of her children were sleeping. She heard the voice again. "Mama!" She looked again in each of her children's rooms, but they were sleeping soundly. Then she looked out the window and saw down the street a child on the corner near the church. She could barely make out the figure under a dim streetlight: a little barefoot boy in short summer pajamas. It was Jack Ellison. How could he have gotten there? She woke up her husband, and they went out to comfort Jack, who was still crying, "Mama . . . Mama!"

After Snow brought Jack home that night, Jack explained that he woke up from a dream that we were going somewhere without him. He looked out the window and saw a passing car. Running to the kitchen door, he turned the handle, the lock in the knob popped outward, and the door opened. He ran after the red car lights to catch us, but he never did. By then he was too confused to know where he was. He saw the church, and thought he could find his way home from it, but was soon lost in the maze of the neighborhood's streets.

As calmly as our jangled nerves would allow, we put Jack to sleep between us that night. I kept one arm and one knee on his little body all night long, and woke up every time he moved. The next morning, Snow stayed home from work and installed dead bolt locks on every outside door, along with a chain lock at the top of each of them. Thanking God together all day, we rejoiced that we had found our lost son, even before we knew he had been lost. With horror, we thought about what would have happened if that car (fantasy or real) driving down our street that night had been going toward the highway instead of deeper into our subdivision of homes, where neighbors would recognize Jack. What would have happened if Mrs. Hellams hadn't heard him, thinking the cry for "Mama" was one of her children? Who else heard his cries? What motives might they have had?

Needless to say, our family grew closer after that incident. We realized the value of our sweet, handsome son, whom—to be honest—we had taken for granted the days before. We cherished every moment with him, his precious sister, and each other. God had given us a miracle of our son, and we had not even recognized it! We also recognized how fragile life is, and how we need to make every moment count. We were never the same. We treasured our family as a gift from God, realizing He watched over us, even though we didn't deserve it.

We are often not aware of God's banner of love and shield of protection over us. We take for granted many of God's blessings every day. We're not able to understand what might have happened if He had not been constantly loving us and caring for us. We don't see all the gifts He gives us, and seldom pause to thank Him for those loved ones and other gifts that are the most precious in our lives. Take time today to thank God for every member of your family. Praise Him that you are wonderfully made (Psalm 139:14), and that you possess blessings every moment that He has provided. Look around you with a thankful heart.

Sometimes we don't recognize blessings we have until we lose them. Then we appreciate more the goodness of God on those days of blessing. Every special blessing has meaning, and we truly know how to thank our Creator! Praise Him today with a renewed heart.

—•••• MEDITATION MOMENTS ••••—

1. Have you ever experienced a pivotal incident that woke you up to the precious gift of life and family God has given you? Reflect on the incident.

2. Name at least ten persons or things for which you are thankful. Now, spend time praising God, the Giver of abundant blessings!

The Three-for-One Special

BY KIMBERLY SOWELL

"Ask, and it will be given to you; seek, and you will find; knock, and it will be opened to you."
—Matthew 7:7 (NKJV)

Driving down old country roads, I turned off the radio to talk with God. *Lord, You know I haven't shared Christ with anyone in a while. I am traveling all day today, stuck in this car, but if there's some way I could be a witness for You, I want to tell someone about Jesus.*

I pulled into the outskirts of my final destination, checked into my hotel, and went next door to Shoney's for supper. As I settled in over a menu, I knew this was my last chance for human contact for the day. *God, I know You heard my prayer,* I thought.

Martina was my waitress, a lovely young lady with an eager smile. When she brought my food and drink, we exchanged small talk and smiles. I told her I was traveling, and she told me about the area. When she picked up my last plate, I asked her a simple question. "Martina, do you ever think about spiritual things?"

A serious look swept over her face. "I have been thinking about spiritual stuff a lot lately. My mother is a Jehovah's Witness and my daddy is a Muslim. I am going off to college in a few months, and I don't know what I believe, but I am trying to figure it out."

Lord, You are so good! "Martina, could I share with you what I have found to be true in my life?" I shared my personal testimony, which included the plan of salvation. Martina had a Bible at home, and she had been reading through the Gospels to learn more about Jesus. "Martina, I know you have to make this decision on your own. I'm glad you have a Bible, and I want to encourage you to keep reading it. Can I also leave a little booklet with my tip that explains how to become a Christian and gives further explanation of what I believe with all my heart, that Jesus is the only way?"

"Oh, yes!" Martina exclaimed. "I would love to have one. Thanks! And I'll be right back with your check."

I pulled a tract out of my pocketbook along with some tip money, and I waited for Martina to return. Moments later, another waitress approached my table. "Excuse me, ma'am. You know that booklet thingy you are giving to Martina?"

"Yes, I have it right here." I held up the tract for the waitress to see.

"Well, she was just telling me about it, and I was wondering, could I have one too?"

"Sure! I'll be glad to give one to you!" Wow! Martina had already told someone else what she had heard about Jesus! It was just like the Samaritan woman who left her pot at the well and went immediately into town to tell everyone about Jesus! The second waitress and I had a brief conversation about the Lord, and she thanked me for the tract, saying it was exactly what she needed.

I could not help but feel the strength of the Lord guiding me, knowing that I had nothing at all to do with these witnessing opportunities; only He could have planted me in this town, in this restaurant, during this work shift, in that section of the restaurant, out of His deep affectionate love for these two lost lambs that He wanted to rescue.

As I rose from the booth to find the register, I greeted the man sitting behind me. "You have a good evening, sir."

"You do the same. Be careful on your long drive home."

I couldn't resist teasing the man, realizing he must have heard me tell Martina I was from out of town. "Were you eavesdropping on my conversation?" He was a tour bus driver, eating alone as his tour group ate on the other side of the restaurant. He seemed to be a kind but lonely man, and he had overheard my conversation with the two waitresses.

The Holy Spirit gently nudged me one more time. "Well, let me ask you the same question, sir. Do you think much about spiritual things?" He replied He was very interested in God, but was unsure about whom to trust. He said he had confidence in Billy Graham and watched him anytime he was preaching on television.

As the older gentleman took small bites and stared into his glass, he confessed that he knew he needed Jesus, but he had never prayed to receive salvation.

I breathed a silent prayer of thanks that the tract in my pocketbook *just happened* to be from Billy Graham, and handing him the tract, I pleaded with him to put off receiving salvation no longer.

God, You are amazing! I asked for one encounter, but You granted three! I got the three-for-one special at Shoney's tonight!

—◆◆◆ MEDITATION MOMENTS ◆◆◆—

1. God is always faithful to provide opportunities for us to minister to others. When was the last time God gave you an unexpected opportunity? How did you respond?

2. We need the sensitivity of the Holy Spirit to allow us to see ministry opportunities in the midst of our busy days, and we also need courage from the Lord to reach out to the lost and hurting. Ask God to grant you spiritual sensitivity, as well as courage, today.

A Month of Miracles

————◆◆◆◆◆◆◆————

Ballerina Dreams

BY MARIE ALSTON

It is better to trust in the LORD than to put confidence in man.
—Psalm 118:8 (NKJV)

My daughter Elizabeth floated across the stage in her white tutu doing her jumps, leaps, and pliés in synchronized harmony with the other girls. She looked like an angel as the snowflakes fell to the stage, bringing closure to the final scene of act 1 of *The Nutcracker*. Seeing her as a beautiful little girl brought back memories to me.

As a young girl I loved to read. I often daydreamed and pretended to be in that faraway or exotic place I was reading about. If there were a heroine in the story, I would become her—a maiden in distress waiting for the knight in shining armor to come and rescue her, or a ballerina. I often escaped my routine, mundane life by imagining myself as the damsel in distress or the heroine in the novel. Most times I dreamed of being a ballerina. I wanted that sleek swanlike neck and petite waist with an hourglass figure. But that was not my lot in life. Unfortunately, I was what some people call "a big girl for my age." When everybody else was a tiny size 2, I was a size 12. Needless to say, I was overly endowed at an early age. I often dreamed of being one of those skinny little girls that looked cute in anything they put on. They seemed to move and dance gracefully to any rhythm, at least in my mind.

Whenever I was with my skinny little friends, I watched from the sidelines while they had a good time on the dance floor. I danced in my head and heart. As Cinderella sang, "In my own little corner in my own little chair, I can be whatever I want to be," in my mind's eye I was a great ballerina. Girl, I could really twirl and dance. Back when I was growing up it was unusual to see a black ballerina in person or on TV. Boy, was I thinking outside the box! But remember, in my book reading I could be anything I wanted to be and go anywhere I wanted to go.

My folks, even though they had limited income (in other words, we were poor), took us on trips every summer during their vacation break from the textile mill. I got to see some of the world outside my immediate surroundings. My parents also encouraged my sisters and me to be whatever we wanted to be. From the spiritual perspective, they taught us that we must put God first in our life, to put our trust in Jesus. From the worldly perspective, they told us to get an education—this could open the door to a whole new world for us.

A Month of Miracles

We all have dreams. But sometimes we find dream-busters in our lives, people who try to squash our hopes and dreams. They tell us what we can't be and can't do because of this reason or that reason. More often than not they are people we know, family and friends, the very people in our lives who say they love us. Yet they don't seem to realize how their comments and putdowns hurt, deterring us from pursuing our dreams.

I never shared my fantasy world with anyone while growing up. It was my childhood safe haven. It was a place where I could go and be whatever I wanted to be or travel wherever I wanted to go. I grew up and moved on with my life. I got my education, found a job, married, and had children. Even though my folks are dead and gone, I still remember what they taught me—to keep God first in my life and get a good education.

No, I did not become a ballerina, nor did I become a great dancer, even though I still love to dance, especially swing dance. However, I do still have a great love for reading. When the pressures of life weigh me down, I curl up with a good book. I block out the world and I begin to read and be whatever I want to be. Jesus did that for me. He took me from a world of mundane life and gave me the greatest miracle of all. He transports all of us from an unfulfilled life in the world and transforms us into miraculous sons and daughters of God!

—•◦• MEDITATION MOMENTS •◦•—

1. What dreams did you have as a child? Share your memories with your family.

2. Do you have unfulfilled dreams in your life today? Do you feel as though life has passed you by? If so, give your heart and life to Jesus and watch a whole new world open up to you.

We Win!

BY CHERIE NETTLES

Ah, Sovereign Lord, you have made the heavens and the earth by your great power and outstretched arm. Nothing is too hard for you.
—Jeremiah 32:17 (NIV)

September 11, 2002—a day that changed our lives. Perhaps you just thought, *Is that a typo? Wasn't it 2001?* Yes, the terrorist attack on America was in 2001; however, the Nettleses' home was forever changed in 2002.

That day I was to begin teaching the Bible study *Lies Women Believe* at my church; it was also the day of my husband's annual checkup. As we met for lunch after his appointment, his cell phone rang. After saying, "Hello," he listened quietly, then said, "Not right now, but what about three o'clock?" He hung up, and it immediately rang again. He answered and said, "This is Mike. Three o'clock at your office, Cardiologists Associates." Mike's tone was urgent. Before he could hang up, I began the inquisition. Mike calmly explained that his EKG (electrocardiogram) revealed a heart abnormality, and he needed to see a cardiologist. I went into my rescue mode, found someone to watch my children, and postponed Bible study. By 4:00 P.M., my husband was admitted to the hospital while I wore a stoic face, and said, "We can do this!"

Within hours, the doctor was talking about "permanent disability." During the next three days, further tests revealed a greater problem, and Mike was scheduled for a heart catheterization. My stoic face melted into tears. On the fifth day, Mike was released from the hospital with five medications he was to take for the rest of his life, and questions about how and when he might return to work. Mike kept insisting he felt fine, but the doctors said he was not.

The next morning, we awoke to a rainy day and another problem. I heard a drip in the den—the roof was leaking! A storm had torn shingles off our roof during the night.

We entered the next week, and Bible study night rolled back around. Attendance was exceptionally high and God truly was at work in many of the women's lives. This study focused on Satan's lies as revealed by Jesus Christ. I had no idea how far Satan would go to stop me from sharing this message from God.

During the third week, my son was playing soccer. His team was winning. Alex ran in to stop an opponent from scoring the tying goal. Alex stopped him all right, but twisted his own ankle. He was carried off the field; we went to the emergency room; and Alex spent the rest of the season on crutches. We seemed to be in a streak of "bad luck."

Entering the following week, I feared what it might hold. As it turned out, week four's crisis was no big deal: just the death of our oven. I called the repairman, who informed me it wasn't just any oven, but a special-order oven to fit into the wall unit of our older home. Ouch! That was costly!

Bible study moved forward. Women began feeling shackles of bondage fall away as they absorbed the truth—there is no condemnation for those in Christ Jesus (Romans 8:2)—and freedom became reality.

Week five arrived, and life seemed to be getting back on track. Mike was back to work, and his heart was stabilizing. We also had a tarp on the roof, and an oven on order. (I like making reservations more than making dinner!)

During week six, I had a speaking engagement. My daughter got strep throat, but fortunately, a simple antibiotic took care of it. What next? I knew not to ask! I awoke Friday morning with a pressure in my right lower abdomen. Too busy to make a doctor's appointment, I called in on the way to the conference, thinking it was a bladder infection. The doctor advised drinking cranberry juice and made an appointment for Monday.

Early into my Monday examination, it was evident I didn't have an infection. By Friday, I was in the oncologist's office. By now, I felt I was going to crumble. Had Satan won? Would he stop me from teaching the Bible study?

Fast-forwarding to today, my husband is well, takes no medications, and is back at work. His heart is normal, though the doctors said this would never happen, and Mike even says it still skips a beat when we kiss. During his heart crisis, Mike said, "Cherie, don't be afraid. I gave this heart of mine to Jesus along time ago, and it's not mine to worry about; it's His. He will take care of me." And that He did!

So—we got a good heart, a new oven, a healthy baseball player (who gave up soccer), a healthy daughter, and a new roof. What about my cancer diagnosis? The Lord had so much more to teach us. Look for that story on day 8 (p.47)! And the Bible study? Satan tried to stop me from teaching, but I didn't stop.

No matter how hard Satan tries to stop us, his lies are revealed through Jesus. Satan didn't win, and he never will. (Just read Revelation!) Trials and suffering sometimes seem bigger than life, but we serve a God for whom nothing is too hard. Satan tried to break my trust in God during those trying weeks, but the Lord gave me the strength to trust. The Lord has given me a testimony, and He has given one to you too. Tell others your story and give Jesus the glory.

(Oh yeah, I love to tell the end of a movie or a book, so I'll go ahead and tell you the end of Revelation: *We win!*)

MEDITATION MOMENTS

1. Do you struggle with sharing your story for Jesus's glory? If so, trust that God has put His words in your mouth and covered you with the shadow of His hand (Isaiah 51:16).

2. Prepare to share by thinking through and writing your story. Then tell a neighbor, a friend, a store clerk, or someone else. Press on. Many more opportunities will come!

————◆◆◆◆◆◆◆————

At All Times and In All Times

By Joy Clary Brown

Trust in him at all times, O people; pour out your hearts to him, for God is our refuge.
—Psalm 62:8 (NIV)

Timing is one of God's greatest miracles. Often the little aggravations of life—the things that slow us down or delay us—are God's ways of protecting us. They are miracles straight from the hand of God. Sometimes we don't recognize these miracles when they happen. Rather, we realize their significance in retrospect.

Such an incident (or as I like to call it, a "God incident,") occurred several years ago when our younger daughter, Molly, and I were in the car. She was driving as we traveled down the highway on a beautiful Myrtle Beach day. Suddenly the "fasten seat belt" light came on, accompanied by the loud sound of a buzzer. We both checked our seat belts and each was fastened. We could find no apparent reason for the warnings.

"What should I do, Mama?" she asked.

I thought for a moment and confessed, "Honey, I honestly don't know. I've never had this happen before. Maybe we should just pull off the road, stop, and turn off the engine." We did, and when Molly restarted the car, the light went off and the buzzer stopped. As we continued down the road, we laughed about how we had "fixed" the car.

Months later a terrible thunderstorm struck the beach one night. Sometime after the worst of the storm had passed, Molly came rushing through the door, drenched with rain, wide-eyed with amazement. She excitedly told us what she had just experienced.

As a college student, she was a leader of the middle-school Fellowship of Christian Athletes (FCA). Her boyfriend's brother was a member of her FCA group, so Molly often gave him a ride home after the meetings.

The remnant of the vicious storm was passing when they got in the car. As they pulled away from the school, the "fasten seat belt" light and the familiar sound of the loud buzzer started again. They each checked their seat belts and found they were fastened.

Molly said, "Once before this happened when I was with my mom. We stopped the car and turned off the engine, and then the light and the noise stopped. I guess we can try that again."

She stopped the car in the parking lot of the school. Upon restarting it, she and Billy were both looking down at the seat belt light. Then it happened. They looked up in amazement and saw the large tree that had just fallen across the road in front of them—the tree that probably would have fallen on the car had they not stopped when the seat belt warnings started.

They sat in silence, realizing the miracle before their eyes. "What ifs" and "almosts" raced through their minds as they praised God for His protective care. After regaining composure, Molly had to drive a long way around the parking lot to avoid the tree lying across the asphalt.

She rushed home to tell us what had happened. We all jumped in the car and headed to the school to see the tree. As we approached the school, we saw emergency vehicles, and the road was blocked to all traffic. We parked the car and climbed on foot to the location of the miracle. The tree was huge and the car was small. We all realized what would have happened if the tree had fallen on the car. With tears of joy we stood at the site and had a prayertime praising God for His protection.

Molly continued to drive that same car for several years. Never again did the light and buzzer come on when the seat belts were fastened. How can that be explained other than a miracle? We praise God for the first time of teaching her to stop the car from the buzzer and lights. We praise Him even more for the second time of using the stopped car to save her life.

Before she went to bed that night, I asked Molly if she thought angels knew how to tamper with cars just enough to turn on seat belt lights and buzzers. We both laughed, but realized anew how timing is one of God's greatest miracles. And this mother will always believe those delays were blessings in disguise!

⟶·•·· MEDITATION MOMENTS ··•·⟵

1. Do you recall an instance when God's timing was part of a miracle in your life?

2. Will you determine to try to see delays as blessings rather than aggravations?

Do You Have a Few Minutes?

By Edna Ellison

Be very careful, then, how you live . . . making the most of every opportunity.
—Ephesians 5:15–16 (NIV)

When I lived in Mississippi, I found a wonderful restaurant that served egg sandwiches. As a widow who lived alone, it was easier, faster, and cheaper—at 89 cents—for me to buy breakfast at that restaurant than it was to buy the eggs, butter, and bread to prepare the meal at home. I began stopping by there every morning on my way to work, hurrying through the drive-through, getting my egg sandwich, and then eating it in the small break room dining area at work before reporting to my desk. Sometimes, at their request, I'd bring an extra sandwich or two for my co-workers, who loved joining me in the break room in the mornings for breakfast.

Running the early-morning shift at the drive-through window was the mother of the family who owned the restaurant, Joan. One morning Joan explained that a year earlier her family had bought the franchise for this restaurant, and since she was an early riser, she had volunteered to work the early-morning shifts. She enjoyed waiting on customers, she said, and knew several of their favorite sandwiches by heart. I grew accustomed to her delicious egg sandwiches and looked forward to talking with her every morning. Joan began to recognize my voice on the speaker system, and often asked before she saw my car or face, "The usual, Edna?"

One morning I found out she was a widow like me, so we found much in common. We talked often, a few seconds at a time, as our drive-through friendship grew.

One Sunday morning I went through the drive-through and startled Joan. She explained that she was not expecting *me*, "one of those Christian types," to come through on a Sunday morning.

She said, "Since I work seven days a week, I never go to church." Then she smiled awkwardly and said, "I always thought a Christian like you would look down on me. I don't really live a righteous life. I guess you'd call me a sinner." She looked down at her feet.

I was about to explain that I was a sinner, too, saved only by God's grace, when I thought of Romans 3:23 (NIV): *"All have sinned and fall short of the glory of God."*

Oh, my goodness, I thought to myself. *I'm already into Scripture verses for the plan of salvation, and I have only a few seconds at this drive-though. Do I dare begin sharing with her? Can I complete a witness in a fast-food spot like this—from my car to her window?* I hesitated. Then I looked out my rearview mirror to see if anyone in the drive-through line was urgently hoping I'd move along.

No cars were behind me, so I began telling her about Jesus. Whispering a quick prayer, I went through the whole plan of salvation, looking deeply into her eyes. No one came up behind me in the usually busy line. She listened intently.

At the end of the Scriptures I shared with her, I asked, "Is there any reason why you wouldn't want to accept Jesus into your heart right now?"

To my surprise, she replied, "Oh, no reason at all. I'd like to—I'd love to—ask Him into my heart, right now!" I led her in a prayer, in which she admitted she was a sinner as all of us are, asked God to forgive her, and told Him she would live for Him every day for the rest of her life. Then she accepted Him as Savior, opening her heart to His presence! She looked like the happiest woman in the world!

I ran a close second, as I grinned in my car!

No joy touches a Christian more than leading someone else to know the Living Lord.

About that time, in God's perfect timing, someone drove up behind me in the drive-through line. I moved forward, promising Joan to keep in touch. I was late for Sunday School that morning, but it didn't matter. I had experienced a miracle of God!

As I contemplated the touch of the Almighty during that brief encounter, I realized that the miracle was not that He saved Joan, but that He performs a miracle every time *anyone* is saved, whether the witnessing time is short or long. The cleansing power of His presence in a human life is the greatest miracle of all.

God taught me that Sunday morning that we, as witnessing women, should be sharing with others in *every* place we go—even in a fast-food drive-through line! May all of us become aware of opportunities in unlikely places. God can perform miracles, even when we believe they are impossible.

⟶•∙∙• MEDITATION MOMENTS •∙∙•⟵

1. Just think! God has the power to take all your mistakes, bad habits, shady past, hurt, suffering, abuse, neglect, and mistreatment—all those things for which humans are ashamed—and He completely wipes them away! Spend a few moments now thanking God that He sent His Son, Jesus, to sacrifice Himself, taking upon Himself all our sins, mistakes, and hurts. Ask Him to fill you with His indwelling Holy Spirit, which will enable you daily to live for Him. Ask Him for a deep sense of the joy of your salvation. Then trust Him to send the joy every day. Write a prayer of praise, affirming your salvation.

A Month of Miracles

2. God also has the power to magnify your natural talents, spiritual gifts, and learned skills so that you can share what you know about Him with others. Ask Him to give you something to say so that you will be able to witness, in an easy, everyday way, according to your lifestyle. Praise Him now for His goodness and His promise never to leave you, but to be with you always (Deuteronomy 4:31), holding you by His strong hand (Isaiah 42:6) as you become a part of His miracles.

———◂◂◂◆◆◆▸▸▸———

A Change of Heart

BY KIMBERLY SOWELL

Whom have I in heaven but You? And there is none upon earth that I desire besides You.
My flesh and my heart fail; but God is the strength of my heart and my portion forever. . . .
But it is good for me to draw near to God; I have put my trust in the Lord God,
that I may declare all Your works.
—Psalm 73:25–26, 28 (NKJV)

Everyone loves Christmas. Candy canes, snowmen, delicious food pleasing to the eye . . . and oh, the joy of experiencing Christmas through the eyes of a child. As I watched the children's Christmas musical at church, I giggled when the little boy down front made faces at his big sister in the audience, and when the little brunette tugged at her stockings for the fourteenth time. But another emotion was welling up deep within me, and I couldn't hold back the tears. Parents of the children in the production filled the pews in front of me. They clapped and cheered for the sheer pleasure of watching their children perform, but I knew I might never experience that joy. Five years of marriage, and my body still wasn't cooperating with efforts to have a child.

After running every medical test and trying every fertility drug available, the specialist declared me a healthy woman, but no treatment was able to make me ovulate. My eggs were stubbornly staying put, and nothing that I could do or that medical innovation could do was going to change reality.

The months of fertility testing had been a roller-coaster journey of faint hopes sandwiched between bitter disappointments. I counted the days on the calendar; I counted the pills in the treatment regimen; and the counting only led to more anxiety, more tears, and more broken dreams. I had read of people going through stages of mourning over the loss of a loved one, and as if death had visited my door, I mourned the loss of what might have been. I asked questions no one could answer, no one except God. I wondered if sins in my past were now punished in my present, leaving me barren. I knew God well enough to know these thoughts were ridiculous, but they still haunted me. Or did God think I was too selfish to be a mother? I compared myself to other women who had babies, and I felt so unworthy of motherhood. Or could it be—what a struggle to say it aloud in my mind—God simply didn't plan for me to be a mother?

I'd heard all my life, *prayer changes things*. I carefully studied 1 Samuel 1 and scrutinized the actions and attitudes of Hannah. I tried to emulate her fervency in prayer. I cried out to God, and lived out the edict to *pray without ceasing*

(1 Thessalonians 5:17). I was praying for a miracle and expecting it to come in the form of two lines on a pregnancy test.

As the months passed, nothing changed. My thoughts, my prayers, and my very will were consumed with having a baby. How was God going to answer my prayers? The deafening silence from above left me feeling brokenhearted and incomplete.

One evening while having a talk with God about a very different subject, being a witness for Christ, I recited my "theme verses" for evangelism: "And He has made from one blood every nation of men to dwell on all the face of the earth, and has determined their preappointed times and the boundaries of their dwellings, so that they should seek the Lord" (Acts 17:26–27 NKJV). Suddenly, God revealed a new application to my heart. God had placed me on this earth at a strategic time and place because He wanted me to seek *Him*. *He* wanted to be the object of my consuming thoughts and prayers. He created my soul to long for *Him*, rejoice in *Him*, rest in *Him*. I had done it again. As had been the case with so many other desires in my life, I had pursued having a baby more vigorously than I had pursued having a deep relationship with God.

I started a fresh search in God's Word. As I studied Hannah's story more carefully, I realized she was made whole before Samuel was ever conceived. Hannah visited the temple, earnestly cried out to God, and after talking with Eli the priest, Hannah "went her way and ate, and her face was no longer sad" (1 Samuel 1:18 NKJV). Hannah's heart was healed and her burden lifted before she rose from her kneeling postition, because she was satisfied that the God who loved her soul was trustworthy to have her best interest in mind as He fashioned her days.

The preceding verses from Psalm 73 offer great encouragement to all who feel disappointment. People, even family, come into our lives and move on, but our God will be with us forever. Our bodies and our attitudes may fail us, but God will never fail to be perfect. Joy is found in nearness to God, and our lives then reflect His wonderful ways.

Instead of healing my womb, God healed my heart. He taught me that the completion I lacked was fulfilled in Christ. What a relief to realize my identity in Christ was not substandard, though I was a wife without a child. My heart returned to gladness to know that as long as I pursue my God, He will pen the details of my life with more splendor and beauty than I could have ever fashioned. God showed me He had plans for me, to give me a future and a hope, if I would only seek Him (Jeremiah 29:11–13). I couldn't wait to see what God had for my future.

━━•◆• MEDITATION MOMENTS •◆•━━

1. Do you have a longing of the heart? Has that longing overtaken God's rightful place as your top priority?

2. In what ways are you actively pursuing a deeper walk with Christ?

Think Pink

BY KIMBERLY SOWELL

"For with God nothing will be impossible."
—Luke 1:37 (NKJV)

Crack! The batter was running, the ball was rolling, and I was yelling. "Hit me! Hit me!" I stood on the dirt behind second base, yelling to the outfielder to throw me the ball. She did just what I asked for—she threw the ball and hit me, literally, right in the chest!

I felt sore for much of the next day. That night when the team gathered to play again, I teased the outfielder about her hard throw to my chest. "My chest has hurt all day because of you!"

"Oh, that means you might be pregnant!" I wasn't thrilled at her method of teasing, because she knew of my infertility. I had driven the desire for a child to the back of my mind, and I was on the road to acceptance when she threw a reminder into my path.

My husband dismissed her comment, but the suggestion lingered in my mind. That night, I hesitantly administered a pregnancy test and was shocked by the viewfinder. The faintest hint of a second pink line showed through the plastic covering. "Hey Kevin, look at this! Can you believe it? These tests are 99 percent accurate, and I happen to buy the 1 percent defective product."

We carefully scrutinized the viewfinder under several lightbulbs, straining to discern two definite pink lines. "Kevin, wouldn't it be amazing if I really were . . ."

"Kim, . . . let's not even talk about it. We've gone down that road before."

"Well, I'll just take another test in the morning and be done with it." We went to bed, and somehow I managed to fall asleep.

The next morning, I took a second test. Once again, the faintest trace of a second line appeared. Could it be? I called the 1-800 number on the side of the box. I informed the customer service operator, "I just took one of your tests. The faintest hint of a second pink line is showing, and I wanted to know if that means I'm pregnant."

"Yes, ma'am, you're pregnant."

"Well, I mean, the line is barely there. It's practically nonexistent."

"Ma'am, it doesn't have to be a dark line. You're pregnant."

"Well, I just want to make sure you're sure. Are you saying there's no way I am not pregnant?"

"You're pregnant."

A Month of Miracles

I hung up the phone and called my husband, then scheduled an afternoon doctor's appointment for a second opinion.

In the hours of waiting for the appointment, I experienced every emotion on the spectrum. I was embarrassed by my behavior with the operator, certain she thought I was unstable, but I felt it inappropriate to discuss my fertility issues with a complete stranger. Well, at least not over the phone. I lay on my bed and opened the Word. I wanted to talk with God, but only gibberish was coming out. I struggled for a coherent thought. Praying for God to send me to the right place, I opened my Bible to Psalms. The words on the page read, "Why are you cast down, oh my soul? And why are you disquieted within me? Hope in God, for I shall yet praise Him for the help of His countenance" (Psalm 42:5 NKJV). God's question to me was legitimate: why was I feeling anxiety and fear?

God had taught me to be content with being childless, and I was OK with my current state two days ago, so why the change in attitude now? I then returned to an old familiar friend, pouring over Hannah's song in 1 Samuel 2:1–10. As I reached verse 10, a warm gush of heavenly love overwhelmed my soul. The words of Hannah were true praise to God. I could agree with every one of her statements, whether or not I was pregnant. My heart did rejoice in the Lord (v. 1). God was my rock, tried and true (v. 2). I knew I was victorious in Christ (vv. 3–4). I had experienced productivity and fruitfulness through God (v. 5). God had given *me* new life (v. 6). I felt rich and favored by God (v. 7). God had lifted me up to a high place with Him (v. 8). I had been blessed under God's protective wing (vv. 9–10). I closed my Bible and knew I was blessed beyond measure, no matter how many lines showed up in the viewfinder.

Appointment time finally arrived. As the nurse called my name, I walked to the door as if on a death march. I knew I was about to take a pregnancy test for the third time, and I had performance anxiety. My nurse laughed out loud when I told her about the first two tests and the call to the company's customer service operator. "Kimberly, we're giving you the same test you've already taken twice. It's going to produce the same results."

"Well, I won't feel pregnant until the doctor says I'm pregnant. I have to know for sure."

I waited for what seemed like hours to get the results from a three-minute test. The nurse looked at the viewfinder and announced, "You're pregnant!" The doctor confirmed it—two pink lines.

Eight months later, Baby Julia entered the world. God didn't have to open my womb, but He chose to open it, according to His timing. I may never know all the reasons why God placed Julia into our home, but God has a reason for everything He does.

The wonderful thing about a miracle is knowing that God is still wonderful, mighty, merciful, loving, and kind, even when He chooses to say no to our requests. That's the kind of God we serve.

━━● MEDITATION MOMENTS ●━━

1. Does your soul feel cast down? How can you replace your sorrow with hope in God? Begin to praise Him right now.

2. Though God doesn't choose to grant our every request, truly nothing is impossible for Him. Have you considered the hopeless feeling you would have if you prayed to a God who had limitations? Thank God for being so mighty that He can do all things.

━◆━◆◆◆◆◆◆◆━◆━

In and Out of My Arms

BY KIMBERLY SOWELL

"My grace is sufficient for you, for My strength is made perfect in weakness."
—2 Corinthians 12:9 (NKJV)

He smelled so enchanting. Resting in my arms was the most precious little boy I had ever dreamed to call my son.

Our miracle daughter was a delight to our souls, and we thanked God daily for Julia, but Kevin and I felt the Lord would make us a family of four. My doctor said I shouldn't expect to get pregnant again, so Kevin and I began to consider adoption. We chose an adoption agency and requested a baby boy from Guatemala. We climbed aboard the paper train of legal documents, waiting daily to hear news we were one step closer to bringing home our son, Jay.

Though the paperwork was still months from completion, I longed to hold my son. I made arrangements to travel to Guatemala, and was granted permission to keep Jay for an entire weekend. What splendor! He was more beautiful than any picture could have conveyed. His hair was soft, his gaze was fetching, and snuggling him in my lap was a dream come true. Throughout the weekend, I obsessed over keeping him within sight and reach, and now, there he lay, sleeping beside me, on our last night together.

Though exhausted, I could not sleep. I didn't want to lose a single moment of watching him, if even to watch him sleep. A single lightbulb burned in the room, just enough to cast a soft shadow of me, his mother, over his tiny frame. I stole my eyes away from him only for brief seconds, glancing at my greatest enemy of the weekend, the clock. Time was passing quickly through the night.

My mind turned back to the first moment I laid eyes on him. He covered just a few square inches on my computer screen, but his photo captured my heart. My husband and I looked at him, pictured as a tiny bundle of newborn, wrinkled flesh, and somehow we knew we would love him for the rest of his life.

I recalled my anxious emotions as I saw the lawyer pull up in her hatchback on that beautiful Guatemalan street just two days earlier. I was about to touch my son for the first time. Jay, the little boy who would grow to be a man in my home, who would cause me to sit in bleachers on scorching afternoons to watch him kick up dust in his little ball uniform, who would need me to clean his scrapes, wash his jeans, and frame his accomplishments on the bedroom wall—the boy who would be a part of my life forevermore, and I was seconds away from laying my eyes upon him for the first time. Those first few moments were bittersweet, because my mind and heart were battling each other. My thrill of holding precious Jay was tainted from the beginning with the sickening pain of knowing it was just for the weekend; in a matter of hours, I would have to give him back into someone else's arms, board a plane, and wait for an undetermined number of months before I could hold my son again.

Light began to appear through the windowpanes, the evidence that morning had come. I no longer could fight my terrified feelings. I wanted to pray, but the pain was heavy. I placed Jay safely in his carrier and lay prostrate on the cold tile floor beside my bed. *God, how can You expect me to do this thing? How can I place my son into someone else's arms, a total stranger to watch over my child?* I knew it would happen one way or another; I had no choice in the matter. *God, I want to glorify You in this morning's exchange, but I don't have the strength. I want to fall apart now; I can't bear to be strong.*

Then I heard the voice of the Lord in my heart. *Kimberly, I have been taking care of Jay from the moment he entered the womb. I have had my hand of protection upon him since the day he was born, and I will continue to keep Jay in my care until you bring him home with you.* A rush of reassurance flooded every empty space in my heart. *And Kimberly, remember, once you get Jay home, he will still be in my care.*

The morning fully bloomed, the lawyer arrived to retrieve Jay, and I watched her drive away with my precious cargo. I shed a mother's tears, but the Lord kept a strong hand upon my shoulder as I placed my final kisses upon Jay's soft cheeks.

On the tile floor of a guest room in Guatemala, did God do a miracle? The sun did not turn back, and time did not stand still. The lawyer didn't miraculously show up with paperwork in-hand to announce I could just take Jay home with me that day. God's capable hands didn't overturn any laws of nature. But what *did* happen was God allowed me to do something I never could have done on my own. Like Samson breaking the temple pillars in his final act of life, or Noah tending an ark full of animals for several weeks afloat, God supplied the necessary strength to my soul at just the right time. Sometimes the miraculous is not what God performs in nature but what He accomplishes in our hearts.

—••••• **MEDITATION MOMENTS** •••••—

1. Have you heard the voice of God lately, telling you to let go of something or someone you are desperately holding on to? How are you responding to God?

2. Daily living requires inner strength. The portion of strength we need is often beyond our capability, helping us realize how deeply we need God. Ask God to give you strength for today's trials; then rise with confidence in His faithfulness to respond.

A Month of Miracles

A Sweet Gift of Love

By Joy Clary Brown

And now these three remain: faith, hope and love. But the greatest of these is love.
—1 Corinthians 13:13 (NIV)

The gray sky served as a backdrop for the dreary day. A cold chill ran through me as I stepped into the shoe repair shop in the small mountain town where we lived. It was sprinkling rain, but it looked and felt as though the snow would begin any moment.

That afternoon's visit to the shoe shop was but one stop on a list of errands I needed to run that day. Little did I realize the blessing that waited for me inside the store.

As I entered, I noticed a beautiful dog reclining on the floor. I immediately was drawn to her and began playing with her. Her beauty was surpassed only by her friendliness. She rolled over for me to pat her tummy, wagged her tail, and acted as though she had been waiting for me all day.

I complimented the storeowner on her pet and she began to tell me her story. She started by explaining, "You have to know that my husband was the sweetest man who ever lived."

The *was* alerted me to the fact that he must be deceased.

She continued, "I had a dog for 12 years who was like my baby. I loved that dog so much. When she died, I felt I could not stand it. It was like I had experienced the death of a family member.

"Two weeks after our dog's death, my husband decided to take me on a trip to try to cheer me up. We were on the outskirts of Hershey, Pennsylvania, when suddenly he looked at me and said, 'I love you.' With that, he drove off the freeway onto the shoulder and slumped over.

"I screamed for help and quickly someone called an ambulance. We made it to the hospital, but my husband died shortly thereafter from a massive heart attack."

She explained how the following weeks were hard even to recall. Grief seemed to be choking the very life out of her. Two of the most precious beings in her life were now gone. She went through the motions of life and tried to move ahead, but she felt stuck in a cycle of loneliness and sorrow.

Forcing herself to go back to work at least gave her a reason to get up in the mornings. One day she was working around the shop when she looked up and saw a lady standing in the doorway holding a puppy.

A Month of Miracles

"Ma'am," the lady announced, "I've come to bring you your puppy."

"What do you mean, *my* puppy?" she replied angrily. "You don't know what you're talking about. My dog died six weeks ago. My husband died a month ago. Get that thing out of here. I don't want anything else around me that I might lose. I couldn't stand to go through another death!"

The lady stood patiently, holding the puppy in her arms, listening as the storeowner vented her emotions. When the gush of anger had come to a halt, the lady explained.

"Ma'am, this really is your puppy. Your husband knew how sad you were over the loss of your dog, so right before you left to go on your trip, he came to pick out a new puppy for you. He asked that we deliver it to you as soon as it was old enough to be weaned. Ma'am, this is your puppy with love from your husband."

With tears streaming down my face, I looked once again at the dog lying on the floor. This time I not only saw a beautiful pet, I saw a miracle.

When I left the shop that day, the sky was just as gray. The air was just as frigid. The rain was just as cold. However, it no longer seemed to be a dreary day. It was a day in which a man I did not even know had blessed me immeasurably. A beloved husband had not only left a legacy of love, he had left a tangible gift of that love.

I returned to the shop one day to ask a simple question. "I just have to know. Did you name the dog . . . "

Before I could finish my question the shop owner smiled and said, "Of course. I named her Hershey." Hershey, what a sweet gift of love!

1. Have you ever realized that simply hearing the story of your acts of kindness can bless the life of a person you may never meet?

2. What legacy are you leaving for others as you journey through life?

Magnolia Miracle

By Edna Ellison

"Here I am! I stand at the door and knock."
—Revelation 3:20 (NIV)

It began as an extraordinary weekend. My only daughter, Patsy, was getting married on Saturday, June 17, 1989. I had worked for months to see that all details were in place: making many visits to our local florist for bride's and bridesmaids' bouquets, groomsmen's boutonnieres, and church sanctuary decorations, and then to a different florist for decorations for a reception hall in Newberry, 30 miles away, where Patsy and her fiancé, Tim, were going to be married. The church was across the street from her new home—and down the road from the site of her first full-time job. My florist suggested I could save money by borrowing flowers from my friends and taking them to Newberry. I knew many friends who had lush magnolia blossoms in bloom, so I arranged to pick up a carload of magnolias the night before the wedding. Tim and Patsy offered to help me place them at the front of the sanctuary.

Walking the bride down the aisle was no problem. My son, Jack, offered to do that, since his father had died about five years before. He teased Patsy and said he'd wanted to give her away since she was about three.

Tim's aunt wanted to bake the wedding cake, and I feared it might be covered with plastic columns or a cheap bride-and-groom figurine that would topple over in the middle of the reception. Then she told me she would place white rosebuds on the layers, and I had a new fear: that ants or other insects would climb out and walk on the cake just as we sliced it for guests! (I shouldn't have worried; it was delicious, and I later learned that she is a master chef!)

I also worried about the chocolate groom's cake, Patsy's dress, the spelling on the engraved napkins, the reception chef's white hat, the way he carved the roast, the ice for punch, the minister's on-time arrival, and all the other little details of the day.

The night before the wedding, Tim's parents provided a wonderful rehearsal dinner, and afterwards Patsy, Tim, and I banked the choir loft in the sanctuary with beautiful magnolias. When we left that night, the sanctuary was a wonderland of large white flowers and slick green leaves. Before we left, we set the air conditioner on a low temperature so the flowers would be fresh overnight.

The next day, while Patsy dressed, Tim and I went to check on the flowers. As we opened the sanctuary door, a gust of hot air hit us. (We found out later that an evening electrical storm had knocked out the air conditioner.) To my surprise, all the flowers were black! Funeral-black, dead flowers!

Tim asked me to go out into the community to get more magnolias and he'd help me place them as soon as he put his cummerbund on his tuxedo. I left quickly, jumping into my car, searching for white magnolias. I could see trees in the distance with white tops. I stopped before the trees with beautiful magnolias. I prayed for three things: safety across the yard (without a vicious dog that might emerge from the bushes and bite my leg), a nice person who would answer the door, and a willing magnolia donor without a shotgun when I asked to rip his tree to shreds!

The older man who came to the door seemed nice enough. No shotgun. No dog. He climbed a stepladder and handed me armloads of magnolia boughs. As I placed the last bunch in my car, I said, "Sir, you have made the mother of a bride very happy."

He said, "No. You don't understand what's going on, do you?"

Before I could answer, he said, "You see, my wife of 67 years died on Monday. We received friends at the funeral home on Tuesday. On Wednesday . . ." He paused.

Swallowing hard, he said, "On Wednesday, I buried her.

"On Thursday my out-on-town relatives went back home, and Friday—just yesterday—my children went back to their homes in Greenwood. This morning, I was sitting in my dark living room, crying out loud. I said to God, *Who needs an old, wore-out, 86-year-old man? Nobody!*

"Then," he said, "You immediately knocked on the door and said, 'Sir, I need you!' When I opened that door, light flooded the room around your head. Are you an angel?"

I assured him I was no angel.

Then I listened as he told all his ideas for a flower ministry, giving his magnolias and also daisies to those who needed encouragement in the neighborhood!

I believe God performed a miracle that day. He knew I could encourage His 86-year-old child, so He moved me out of the church and into the world by sending the storm to destroy my flowers. Then He sent me to the home of His child, in His timing.

God often coincides His will with our needs—performs miracles for His glory!

——•••• MEDITATION MOMENTS ••••——

1. Has a need in your life led you to another person that needed your encouragement? What happened?

2. God often leads us—unexpectedly—to be His spokespersons as we open new doors. He also says in the end of Revelation 3:20, today's opening verse, "If anyone hears my voice and opens the door, I will come in and eat with him, and he with me." As you pray, ask God to fellowship with you today and allow you to encourage others to fellowship with Him.

3. Do you have a humorous or disastrous story about a family wedding? Share it with a friend or study partner, and tell how God worked out all the details.

A Month of Miracles

——◆◆◆◆◆◆◆◆◆◆——

Victory Scars

BY MARIE ALSTON

In the same way, the Spirit helps us in our weakness. We do not know what we ought to pray for, but the Spirit himself intercedes for us with groans that words cannot express. And he who searches our hearts knows the mind of the Spirit, because the Spirit intercedes for the saints in accordance with God's will.
——Romans 8:26–27 (NIV)

As I heard a horrible piercing scream echo down the hallway, my immediate "mama thought" was *Oh, my God! That's a real cry, not a fake one.* We mothers just seem to be able to tell the difference. As I raced toward the screams and cries, my mind went back to the few minutes earlier when I had allowed my five-year-old son Joshua, and my four-year-daughter Elizabeth to jump on my bed. For some reason all children seem to enjoy bed-jumping. As they jumped, I could hear them chanting the little nursery rhyme: "Five little monkeys jumping on the bed; One fell off and bumped his head. Mama called the doctor and the doctor said, "'No more monkeys jumping on the bed.'"

I figured this would entertain them while I went back into the kitchen to finish preparing dinner. Little did I know that they had gone from just jumping up and down on the bed to climbing onto the top of the dresser and jumping off onto the bed. While racing, pushing, and shoving each other to be the first to climb back up on the dresser, Elizabeth's foot slipped behind the dresser, coming in contact with the jagged edge of a broken mirror that I had stored there until I could have it repaired and mounted on the back of the bedroom door.

As I opened the door, I could see blood gushing from the top of her foot. I grabbed her, lifting her up, raced into the bathroom, ran cold water over her foot, wrapped it in the wet towel, and then double-wrapped it again in a dry towel. The whole time I wrapped, I was praying, *Lord God, please don't let her bleed to death; please don't let her bleed to death!*

I grabbed the keys off the counter, put her and my other three children in the car, and off we headed to the emergency room. As I hurried with Elizabeth in my arms into the emergency room door, a nurse met me and took Elizabeth out of my arms. Screaming, I cried over my baby, trying to tell the nurse what had happened to her. She immediately took Elizabeth to a back room, where a doctor went to work on her foot, trying to get the gushing bleeding to stop. She had a two-inch-deep gash on the top of her left foot. The doctor told me that she had missed a major artery by a small distance. If the cut had hit that artery, Elizabeth would have bled to death before we could have helped her. He predicted that she would need a skin graft from her thigh to cover a hole that size.

In the meantime, the staff had called Dr. Au, a local plastic surgeon, to come for a second opinion.

At this point, I started to lose what calm had remained inside. I felt helpless to do anything for my child. I began to pray, but the words would not form. I could only moan and groan in prayer. The Scripture that came to my mind was Mark 11:24, "Therefore, I tell you, whatever you ask for in prayer, believe that you have received it, and it will be yours" (NIV).

Dr. Au came in, took one look at Elizabeth's foot, and spoke to the nurse in whispers. I imagined the worst. She came back with a tray of instruments and tools for Dr. Au. He told me to hold Elizabeth. Then—wonder of wonders—he began to stitch up that hole in her foot! I was watching a gigantic answer to prayer, a miracle unfolding right before my very own eyes! I could hardly believe what God was doing though Dr. Au!

Elizabeth did not have a skin graft, nor does she have any trouble walking on that foot. And to this day, the only evidence she has is the scar from the stitches on the top of her foot.

I believe Satan tries to hurt and destroy us. He will use whatever means necessary—circumstances, situations, joys, or even the people we love so dearly in our lives—to bring us terror. He makes us fear the worst, but God is still in control, blessing us in miraculous ways.

This experience with Elizabeth was a milestone in my life. It left a scar in my heart because of the trauma, but it's a victory scar, reminding me of God's goodness and healing miracles.

A few years ago, a friend and her husband, a minister, were in a terrible car accident in which she was thrown from the car. After searching for some time, the rescue team found her, badly broken up, with cut glass in her forehead and cheeks where she had landed in the broken window glass, face first. When I saw her sometime later at a ministry function, she shared about how her doctors told her that she could have plastic surgery to remove a large scar on her cheek. She decided to leave the scar as it was. When she looks in the mirror today, it reminds her of God's goodness and that He is still in control. She said, "Satan tried to kill me, but God said, 'Not so.' Satan meant it for bad, but God meant it for my good."

Sometimes all of us are hurt by the devil, whether we followed in his way willingly or unknowingly. We are hurt by sin and evil things that happen to us. However, God can bring complete healing as we turn our situations over to Him.

⟶⟶ MEDITATION MOMENTS ⟵⟵

1. Stop and think about a time that you felt utterly helpless. When was the last time you tried to pray for someone and could only moan, unable to pray clearly? Thank God for hearing our prayers and bringing His presence and mercy into our lives during such times.

2. You'll probably never know how much people around you need prayer. Think of someone who might need prayer today. Intercede on his or her behalf.

A Month of Miracles

———◆◆◆◆◆◆◆◆◆————

Beautiful Feet

BY CHERIE NETTLES

How beautiful are the feet of those who bring good news!
—Romans 10:15 (NIV)

Beautiful feet? What? Suitors have told me many things in my lifetime, but never that my feet were beautiful. In fact, anyone who said that would be lying! My feet were never pretty, but by age 17 there was no *beauty* in them. Don't get me wrong, I'm thankful for my feet; I'm just hoping they're not my best feature!

At age 17, I awoke late one December evening to the ring of the telephone. I jumped out of bed and ran through the den, and—bam!—right into the hearth of the fireplace. (Running while groggy is not recommended. And if the furniture has been rearranged for the Christmas tree, you really need to be alert and turn on a light, because smacking your toes on the bricks of a hearth really hurts.) I hobbled to the telephone, and wouldn't you know it, the caller had hung up. I hobbled back to my bed, and took a minute to drift back to sleep because of the throbbing in my toes.

Little did I know that night would change the rest of my life; I spent the next two years in and out of doctor's offices, hospitals, and clinics trying to figure out why the inflammation and pain would not subside. Finally, two years and many medications later, I landed in the office of a rheumatologist, a doctor that treats arthritis and other autoimmune diseases. By this time the pain and inflammation had migrated up my right leg into my knee. My knee was so swollen I couldn't pull my straight-leg jeans over it, and for a girl of the 1980s, that was a tragedy. I began to hurt everywhere in my body. My doctors seemed to believe it was some form of arthritis, but they didn't know what kind. None of my blood work was conclusive. The arthritis appeared to be rheumatoid, but I didn't seem to fit the profile.

After months of treatment, my disease progressively worsened. I withdrew from college and spent most of my 19-year-old days in bed. I felt hopeless. During one of my routine appointments, my doctor explained that my disease had become aggressive, and I needed to prepare for my future. His prognosis was that by age 21, my disease would cripple me, and I would live the remainder of my life in chronic pain in a wheelchair.

I left his office sobbing, feeling my life was over. I asked God why! My dreams of college, becoming a teacher, a wife, and a mother were over. How could God allow this to happen to me? I couldn't become pregnant while taking high-risk medications, and my doctor predicted I would never be able to stop taking these medications.

A Month of Miracles

Five surgeries, 27 years, and multiple regimens of high-risk, long-term medications later, I'm still walking! Oh, my toes are deformed, and I walk with a pronounced limp, but I walk! My feet aren't beautiful, but they still take me where I want to go. And about my dreams: in 1984, I graduated cum laude from the University of South Carolina (Go Gamecocks!) with a degree in education. I became a teacher and, in 1989, married the man of my dreams. In 1990, my disease went into a five-year remission, and during that time I came off all of my medications. I was given the OK to try to have a baby. And guess what? In February 1991, I gave birth to the most beautiful baby boy ever. Then in 1993, I gave birth to the most beautiful baby girl ever! Wow! (If you don't believe me, I could mail you a thousand pictures to prove it.) God is a God of miracles. I prayed for more than 12 years about having children, and had I known the wonder God was going to bestow on me with my two children, I would have prayed longer! God is our Great Physician, and He can do what man cannot.

You may be suffering today from physical or emotional pain. You, too, may feel that your life is over or that your dreams have been snatched from you. Trust me when I say that God is our Dream Maker. Psalm 37:4 teaches us to delight ourselves in the Lord and He will grant us the desires of our hearts. There is nothing too hard for God. Jeremiah 32:17 says, "Ah, Sovereign Lord, you have made the heavens and the earth by your great power and outstretched arm. Nothing is too hard for you" (NIV). Your life is not over. I'm telling you to keep dreaming not because I've read it somewhere, but because *I've walked it!*

⸺•◆•⸺ MEDITATION MOMENTS ⸺•◆•⸺

1. Today, I'd like you to take this time to reflect upon the words of our Dream Maker. Below are some verses I've clung to in times of suffering. Look up each verse and fill in the blanks. (The verses are quoted from the NIV.)

    - Proverbs 3:5–6: "Trust in the Lord with all of your heart and lean not on your own understanding; in all your ways acknowledge him, and he will make your _____ straight."

    - 2 Corinthians 12:9: "My grace is _____ for you, for my power is made perfect in _____ ."

    - 2 Corinthians 4:18: "So we fix our _____ not on what is seen, but on what is unseen. For what is seen is temporary, but what is unseen is eternal."

    - 2 Corinthians 5:7: "We live by _____ not by _____."

May you always walk in the light of His glory!

A Simple Testimony

By Tricia Scribner

"For I did not come to call the righteous, but sinners to repentance."
—Matthew 9:13 (NKJV)

Many people I know have astounding testimonies of conversion to faith in Christ. A friend of mine was delivered instantaneously from heroin addiction when he accepted Christ. I know people who have left prostitution to come to Jesus, and others who have come to Christ while in prison on death row. By comparison, my testimony of conversion seems too simplistic to have accomplished my eternal salvation.

It was 1960, and my family lived in Lake Charles, Louisiana, where my dad was stationed at Chenault Air Force Base. Having become believers in their early years, both my parents had strayed away, until the pastor of the nearby little Baptist church came to talk with them about living their lives for Jesus Christ. They decided to do just that, and I have no memory of anything but my family living faithfully for the Lord.

We were active in the church, and I still remember tiny flashes of experiences there. I recall, for instance, after church one winter Sunday, I backed up to the wall heater a little too closely and walked away to find I had burned stripes across the back of my vinyl coat. I also recall the worship choruses I learned during those early years, such as "Deep and Wide" and "Hallelu, hallelu, hallelu, hallelujah, Praise ye the Lord!" in which we kids divided into groups and jumped to stand when we sang one phrase or the other. One memory stands apart from the others, though, not because it is more clearly imprinted on my mind, but because it is of such great importance.

I was about five years old, and my mom and I sat on the living room couch, when the subject of heaven came up. I felt pretty good about heaven. After all, I thought, it was where good people who loved Jesus went, and that certainly included me. I had been in church as long as I could remember. I loved God and knew He loved me too. My feeling of security was soon to evaporate.

Mom explained that heaven was prepared for believers in Jesus Christ. Everyone had sinned, she said, and sin separated us from God, who was completely good and could not allow sin into heaven. Well, I was five years old. How much could I know about sin? I hadn't killed anyone. And I hadn't robbed any banks. On the other hand, I had to admit, I had hit my sister and made her cry, and I had dug a hole in the plaster wall with my fingernail during naptime. So, there I was, a five-year-old hell-bound sinner, and I knew it.

A Month of Miracles

Fortunately, Mom continued, God had provided a way of salvation for sinners like me, by sending Jesus to die on the Cross to pay for my sin. I knew the story. He loved us so much that He died in our place. Then she explained that Jesus would forgive and give eternal life in heaven to anyone who trusted in Him to become his or her Savior. As my mom and I sat on the couch, I prayed, telling Jesus I knew I had sinned, asking Him to forgive me, and inviting Him to come into my life as my Savior.

Sometimes we forget the astonishing miracle of salvation. Or, maybe we think that a testimony of conversion must be dramatic to be genuine. But my story teaches us at least two miraculous truths about the salvation our God offers. First, whosoever will may come to Him, whether a hardened criminal or a little child. But we must come to Him on His terms. We must first recognize we are sinners by nature and by choice and that we cannot fix our sin problem on our own. You see, as a young child, I loved Jesus as I understood Him. Thousands upon thousands of people believe they are eternally secure because they sincerely love God. But until I recognized that Jesus Himself said I was a sinner and in order to be accepted by God, I had to turn away from my sin to trust Jesus, I was separated from God and without hope.

The second truth we learn from my simple salvation story is that while dramatic testimonies may be compelling, they do not reveal any greater working of God than the testimony of childlike faith. For, as great as it is that God would stoop to snatch someone from a life of horror and degradation, perhaps more amazing is the fact that in His tender grace and through the power of His Holy Spirit, He would stoop to reveal to a five-year-old child her sin and need for the Savior. Now, that's a miracle!

—◆◆◆ MEDITATION MOMENTS ◆◆◆—

1. Dear friend, do you have a testimony of conversion to faith in Jesus Christ as your Savior?

2. If you have already come to faith in Christ, recount to someone how God demonstrated His tender grace by offering you His gift of salvation.

The Blue Shepherd

By Edna Ellison

Now to him who is able to do immeasurably more than all we ask or imagine, according to his power that is at work within us, to him be glory in the church and in Christ Jesus throughout all generations, for ever and ever! Amen.
—Ephesians 3:20–21 (NIV)

Have you ever had one of those days with teenagers that seemed like a comedy of errors from beginning to end? One Sunday morning in the 1960s, I'd cooked and served breakfast, spilled milk in the refrigerator, wiped it out, and was mopping the dribbles off the floor when Jack, our teenage son, needed to iron out a wrinkle. To speed up the process, I set up the ironing board myself, steam-pressed the wrinkle, and creased the pants as quickly as I could. I finally headed out the door, hurrying Jack, his sister, Patsy, 13, and their father to the car. (My wonderful husband was reading the paper.)

Since that morning's Bible study was long, I taught my Sunday School class at a speed of 90 miles per hour, with gusts up to 100! Trying not to seem rushed as a visitor lingered at the door, I then stripped my jacket off as I ran down the hallway and jumped into my choir robe, entering the sanctuary with the rest of the choir. Some of them—good friends—mumbled a joke about changing clothes and "streaking." I laughed and then sang with as much air power as I could muster, but I was tired.

After church, we finished the biggest meal of the week. Two hours and a chicken carcass later, as I washed dishes, Patsy said, "Mom, Mrs. Franklin called yesterday, and we are having a dress rehearsal for the Christmas pageant this afternoon at five o'clock."

I laid the dishcloth down, greasy from the gravy pan.

"Patsy, the Christmas pageant is two weeks away. We'll be ready on time." I longed for the couch and a few minutes' rest.

"But, Mom, tonight is dress rehearsal. Allison is a beige shepherd, and I'm a blue shepherd."

"Surely Mrs. Franklin is not expecting all of you in costumes two weeks before the performance."

"She came in our Sunday School class again this morning and said it's really easy; we just need a blue piece of cloth, with rough edges, no hemming. Just sew, sloping down the shoulders and leave an opening for a boat neckline and armholes, like a caftan." (*Easy for her to say,* I thought to myself.) I looked toward heaven: *Lord, save me from having to sew a shepherd's costume today*, I prayed.

"C'mon, Patsy," I said a few moments later. "Let's see if we have any fabric." We looked in a closet where we stored cloth: pink-flowered piquet, polka-dotted green silk, yellow stripes, but no blue cloth suitable for a shepherd. Then I remembered. Months before, a student had left a bag with blue cloth in my English classroom at the school where I taught. If we could find it, I might whip it into a costume in a few hours, but I was not sure where it was. It lay on a lost-and-found table outside my classroom until the principal asked us to clean up for a PTA meeting. I'd asked a student to put it in a file cabinet, but I had not checked to see where she had placed it.

I called the school secretary to get a key to the school, and Patsy and I headed for her house. On the way, she said, "Oh, yes, Mom. I also need a scarf the same color as the shepherd's robe, and a blue rope to tie around it to make a head cover."

I laughed. "Blue rope! Have you ever seen a blue rope? Impossible!" She laughed, too, and shrugged her shoulders.

We entered the school with the secretary's key and wandered the dark corridors to my room. As we dug into the lost-and-found junk in the file drawers, there it was: a bag with blue polyester cloth. Imagine our surprise when I shook it out and found a flowing caftan: a perfect shepherd's costume, with a boat neckline, sloping shoulders, and loose armholes. Patsy tried it on, and it fit perfectly!

"Look, Mom," she said. She lifted out a scarf that fit, hanging below her shoulders. Then she pulled out the unbelievable: a blue rope, long enough to tie around her head, making a perfect shepherd's head cover!

I don't know how that costume appeared. Did a home economics student sew it months before and then decide that a caftan wasn't her style? Did God miraculously zap it that day in the drawer? I know only that He answered the prayer of a tired mother, who prayed, *Lord, save me from having to make a shepherd's costume today,* and He did it His way—far above anything I had imagined.

·•✦ MEDITATION MOMENTS ✦•·

1. How has God provided for your needs?

2. List some of the "unbelievables" in your life (things God has given you that are unbelievable blessings, more than you dared to hope for). Thank God for His unbelievable power!

—◆◆◆◆◆◆◆◆—

God's Good Thoughts

By Tricia Scribner

"For I know the thoughts that I think toward you," says the Lord, "thoughts of peace and not of evil, to give you a future and a hope. Then you will call upon Me and go and pray to Me, and I will listen to you."
—Jeremiah 29:11–12 (NKJV)

I went to work one morning at our family's frozen yogurt/juice bar business after facing a crisis at home the night before. Our oldest daughter had run away from home during the night, and the police had to be called to help us locate her. I came to work with a tear-stained face, utterly spent and hopeless; I cleaned tables and waited on customers while fighting back tears.

My husband and I had debated and prayed and reprimanded and tried to listen and showed empathy and given boundaries and consequences, and, well, the fact was, nothing had curbed our daughter's increasingly dangerous and self-destructive behavior. I had spent many hours in agonizing prayer to the Lord about how to parent this child whom we loved dearly, but who seemed to have entered our home with her own playbook when we adopted her at age five.

In my times with the Lord, His response to me personally seemed more and more indifferent. I *knew* He deeply cared but I sure couldn't *feel* His presence or His guiding wisdom as I emotionally limped along. But then, I wondered, how could He speak to me when I was so caught up in my own personal self-pity and pain that I couldn't even pray in faith? When it came to meeting Him in His Word, I could hardly decipher the words on the Bible page, much less let their truth sink into my soul.

When the phone rang in the back of the store, I was shaken back to reality. Maybe I could just let it ring. I wasn't up to answering a customer's question about what kind of frosting she wanted put on her perfectly happy and sane daughter's birthday cake. Good manners prevailed, and I picked up the phone and answered with the usual business greeting. It was a friend of mine.

"Hey, Tricia," she said.

I responded in kind, trying to keep my voice from sounding as flat as I felt. I wondered why she would be calling me at work.

She said, "I need help on a Bible question."

Oh, great, I thought, *that's what I need right now, to get quizzed on a Bible question when I obviously know very little Bible truth or we wouldn't be in this mess.*

"OK, I'll try," I muttered.

She continued, "Where is that verse that tells us God thinks good things about us?"

I knew it well, but in the past few weeks its message had gotten obscured behind the veil of sorrow. I had committed Jeremiah 29:11 to memory years before while in Africa serving as a volunteer nurse for several weeks. The verse had been displayed in a cross-stitched picture frame on the wall of the missionaries' home where I had stayed. It became a bold statement of faith when I learned they had lost their only child in an accident while on this missions field just a few years prior. During the days of my volunteer service when I attempted to practice nursing in a place of foreign languages, foreign customs, and foreign diseases, it had reminded me that if these missionaries had endured such a trial and found God faithful, then surely I would find Him faithful in my own trials.

So, I said, "Yes, that verse is Jeremiah 29:11, 'I know the thoughts that I think toward you,' says the LORD, thoughts of peace and not of evil, to give you a future and a hope'" (NKJV). The words were no sooner out of my mouth than tears spilled onto my cheeks.

She said, "Thanks so much."

I responded, "No, thank *you*. You have no idea how much I needed that verse right now."

There are times in our lives when God seems to have turned a deaf ear to our cries of pain and sorrow. We wonder where the moments of divine solace and wisdom have fled, just at the critical time when we need them the most. But, as this experience taught me, our God is willing and able to speak to us even when we've become discouraged and our faith is on shaky ground, even when our minds are numb and we feel unable to absorb His word or hear His voice in prayer.

For a God who will use an unsuspecting friend with a question and the faded memory of a cross-stitched verse displayed in the home of godly suffering servants in Africa—a God who will go to such lengths to speak to the heart of a hurting and faithless child—this God is One who we should never doubt thinks good thoughts toward us.

✦✦✦ MEDITATION MOMENTS ✦✦✦

1. Have you ever endured a trial that caused you to question whether God had your best interest at heart?

2. What did the Lord teach you about His thoughts toward you during that time, or perhaps after the trial had ended?

3. What hope can you offer to friends who are currently enduring a hard trial that has shaken their faith? What hope does God offer you in your trials?

A Month of Miracles

Eighty Dollars

BY MARIE ALSTON

I have no greater joy than to hear that my children walk in the truth.
—3 John 4 (NKJV)

Having four children so close in age meant our schedule was always full with events and transporting children from one activity to another. Perhaps because I had the biggest van or because I had the most children, I became the official taxi for pickup and delivery of the neighborhood kids, who happened to be on the same sports teams or involved in other afterschool activities as my children. Boy, was I looking forward to the day when one of the kids was old enough to get a driver's license.

Our yard was also the official neighborhood playground. We had equipment for every imaginable sport, including basketballs and a goal, soccer balls, softballs, gloves, and bats, to name a few. I've still got the broken windows as memories of those days. My husband was a local pastor, so we looked at the time the kids played in our yard as an opportunity to minister and witness to them. However, we did institute a few ground rules that the kids had to abide by if they wanted to stay and play in our yard:

- Rule 1: No arguing.
- Rule 2: No fighting.
- Rule 3: No profanity (meaning, no cussing).
- Rule 4: No playing in our yard if we were not at home.

The kids usually did very well honoring our rules. Whenever someone slipped out an ugly word or started to argue, we would poke our head out and say, "Whoever said that, you've got to go home." It seemed everybody would say in unison, "Not me, Mr. and Mrs. Alston." We knew they weren't going to tell on their friends, but we would ask anyway, just to let them know we were listening and watching from afar, even if we were in the house.

Our backyard play ministry went fine until my son Emanuel hit his teen years. As he matured, he seemed embarrassed by our intervention when one of the kids broke the yard rules. He also began to exert himself against our authority in everyday conversations, arguing and giving a biting retort when we asked him to do something. He accused us of embarrassing him in front of his friends. He resented our talking about our relationship with God, calling us hypocrites and saying we were not saved because at times we argued or yelled at him. Filled with anger and

A Month of Miracles

bitterness, he hated when we'd tell him he couldn't watch shows on MTV or listen to certain music, such as gangster rap. He seemed to have doubts about who he was and whose he was. Suggesting activities related to church and God met with sure resistance. He didn't need God because, he thought, as playwright Lorraine Hansberry wrote, he was "young, gifted, and black."

We prayed for our son's salvation and that God would keep him in His ark of safety until he was able to see God's power in his life. We asked God to show him concrete miracles to help him believe.

During this time we looked for ways to meet his needs. His junior year in high school, he played on the basketball team. When he needed $80 to pay his coach for his basketball shoes, he came to us. Even though money was tight, we gave him the money with instructions not to flash his money around as though he were rich; just pay the coach. Of course, he thought our warnings were silly. He went to lunch and took his wallet out with the four $20 bills I had given him and showed his friends. Later that afternoon, when he went to the coach's office to pay, he realized his wallet was gone. He called me, crying like a baby. Little did he know that God was at work revealing His love.

The young man who had picked Emanuel's pocket at lunch boarded the school bus that afternoon, bragging to his friends about what he'd done. The boy's cousin, a friend of my daughter Liz, had talked with Liz earlier and had learned that Emanuel's wallet had been stolen. She called the principal and reported that her cousin may have taken the wallet. The principal called the young man's house and confronted him. The boy returned the wallet to the school office the next day, and the principal gave Emanuel his wallet. When Emanuel looked inside his wallet, the four $20 bills were still tucked inside. From that day on, we noticed that Emanuel's spirit mellowed. Even today, I marvel at how God took such great measures to prove His love for Emanuel.

————◆◆◆ MEDITATION MOMENTS ◆◆◆————

1. Recall a time when God went to extraordinary measures to demonstrate His love for you or someone you love. Share how this event strengthened your faith.

2. For whom are you now praying that God will work in unmistakable ways to reveal Himself and His love?

Not Just a Dream

BY TRICIA SCRIBNER

For by grace you have been saved through faith, and that not of yourselves; it is the gift of God, not of works, lest anyone should boast.
—Ephesians 2:8–9 (NKJV)

Daddy had just come on furlough after being gone for six long months, one-half of his yearlong, isolated tour assignment at Greenland's Sondrestrom Air Force Base. Into those few furlough days we had stuffed a lifetime's worth of family memories. My year-younger sister and I talked Daddy's ears off, trying to catch him up on school events, accomplishments, and church happenings. We popped popcorn and watched *Tarzan* on TV. We regaled him with multiple encores of plays in which we starred, each trying to outdo the other.

Most of all, we wanted to show him our newly acquired piano skills. Having graduated from the beginners' books during his absence, we played on our 21-key electric chord organ every new music piece we had mastered, attempted, or even seen once in our John Thompson's piano books. The snaggletoothed renditions were punctuated by blips of silence as our fingers reached for imaginary notes that were printed on the page but not provided on our abbreviated keyboard. Still, Daddy acted suitably impressed at every little run and flurry, and we played with gusto, relying on the premise that all's well that ends loud.

I dreamed of a "real" piano, but an 88-key real piano that didn't have to be plugged in was out of the question on my dad's air force salary. My parents did well just to tithe, buy food, and pay the bills—and they did just that, in that order. It was just as well we didn't have a piano; where would we put it in our little 10-by-55-foot trailer?

The days of furlough we had anticipated for so many months, marked on the calendar, and diligently prayed would come, wound down too quickly. Daddy's impending departure loomed before us as we prepared to take him back to the airport the following day and face another good-bye for six more months.

Despite the intensity of our time together, or perhaps partly because of it, my sister and I bickered incessantly. Our verbal skirmishes seldom accomplished anything except to push my mom into a state of utter frustration as she attempted to arbitrate such disagreements as who touched whom first and who was "gritting her eyes" at whom.

In one such moment on the last day, Mom said, "Girls, go to my bedroom." Boy, were we in trouble now. I mentally reviewed the list of possible sins we could

A Month of Miracles

have committed, but nothing specific, or at least unusual, came to mind. My sister and I plodded back to Mama and Daddy's bedroom and gingerly sat on the edge of the bed.

She began, "Girls, this is your daddy's last day home. Please, don't make it miserable by arguing."

What was that bumping noise?

She went on, "You two have been at each other, and we've just about had enough . . ."

There it went again. A thud, voices, and a scraping sound.

"So, I want you both to work hard at getting along during these last few . . . "

My sister and I couldn't bear it. We bolted for the bedroom door and catapulted into the living room.

It was the most beautiful piano I had ever seen. Liberace had never played on a keyboard so beautiful. Its brown wood gleamed and it boasted a full complement of 88 keys—I counted them. My sister jumped up and down, squealing, "Can I play it?! Can I play it?!" while I stood mute. A real piano had somehow crawled into my living room. Would it leave the same way? One can never be too wary when a mammoth musical instrument only fit for dreams shows up in one's living room. Maybe it *was* a dream.

As my sister plunked the keys, tears crept into my eyes. It was the most precious gift my parents had ever given us; even as a child I could imagine the sacrifice my parents had made in order to purchase the exquisite instrument. With trembling fingers, I reached out and touched it. It was real. And it was mine.

As a believer, sometimes I doubt the precious gift of salvation. After all, it's hard to believe that God Himself would sacrifice His only beloved Son for my eternal life. The whole idea seems like a pipe dream. I don't deserve eternal life any more than I deserved that exquisite piano. And since I didn't deserve salvation, maybe one day, after recounting all my great sins, God will take it back.

But then I remember the day when as a young child I asked Mama if I'd get to go to heaven, and she explained how sin separated me from God, who was as righteous as He was loving. She said He, in fact, loved me so much He gave His only Son to die in my place, and if I asked Jesus to forgive me and trusted Him to save me, He would.

In that moment, knowing Jesus offered the gift to me with His nail-pierced hands, I knew it was more than just a dream. With trembling heart, I reached out and took it. I know it is real. And it is mine.

A Month of Miracles

— ❧❧❧ MEDITATION MOMENTS ❧❧❧ —

1. Have you ever doubted the gift of salvation was real?

2. How does this story explain how a person can receive God's offer of salvation? If salvation is a gift of grace and not of works, what *keeps* believers saved?

Christmas with Daddy

By Edna Ellison

But you received the Spirit of sonship. And by him we cry, "Abba, Father."
—Romans 8:15 (NIV)

Bible scholars tell us *Abba* means "Daddy." Every time I read the end of the verse above, translated "*Daddy, Father*," it brings fresh memories of a time when my daddy was a young man and I was five. That December, God blessed me with a miracle.

During World War II, my father served in the navy. My mother, four-year-old brother Jimmy, and I lived with grandparents while Daddy was gone. We'd hoped he could come home for Christmas 1944, but the situation was looking bleak. With only a short leave, it was doubtful he could make it home by Christmas.

Mother explained that we needed to celebrate a good Christmas even though Daddy might not be able to come home, but Jimmy and I had prayed the night before, asking God to send Daddy home, and we knew God always answered prayer.

Every day, Jimmy and I looked out the window toward the bus station. We watched soldiers and sailors returning for Christmas, but we didn't see our daddy. One day, a man in bell bottoms, a navyblue peacoat, and a white sailor hat headed toward our house! We knew it must be Daddy. Imagine our disappointment when he turned at the corner and went down another street! It wasn't Daddy.

My Aunt Clara, who also lived with our grandparents temporarily, tried to cheer us up. "See how happy Tommy and Ricky are," she said, laughing. I knew her toddlers didn't even remember their father. I could remember my daddy: the smell of his aftershave lotion, the kindness in his brown eyes, and the sound of his clarinet lullaby at bedtime. What fun to bounce among the covers as he calmed us with music! Jimmy and I often lay down at bedtime and Daddy played "one more song" before we went to sleep. We couldn't wait to see him again! We spent many hours watching the street.

On Christmas Eve, Aunt Clara gathered Mother, Jimmy, and me in the living room. "I have a surprise for you," she said. I ran to the door. There on the porch stood Aunt Alice, *only Aunt Alice*, dragging a Christmas tree!

"This tree's too tall," Aunt Clara said, going to the piano. "While Alice saws it, I'm going to play 'Jingle Bells.' We'll sing while she saws." With the trunk of the cedar tree over a large bucket, Alice started sawing. I pouted.

"I thought you were Daddy," I said.

A Month of Miracles

I refused to sing, but when I saw Mother holding hands with Tommy, Ricky, and Jimmy, marching them around the tree, I joined in, halfheartedly. Later Mother said, "Edna, I'm glad you helped the boys march around the tree tonight. As the oldest, you helped them be happy this Christmas. I know it's hard to wait. I'm waiting too."

Awaking on Christmas morning, I began my window vigil. "Why don't you go into the living room . . . see your presents?" Mother said. Jimmy ran quickly. I dawdled. In the living room, I saw two small bicycles beside the tree! And then—Daddy stepped out from behind the tree, welcoming us with open arms! Of many wonderful memories of the past, that was the greatest Christmas of all.

Every Christmas our church celebrates Advent, which means "the coming of something momentous." God gave us the greatest gift when He allowed His Son, Jesus, to live on earth as the Incarnate Christ. His birth was the coming of something momentous—a miracle of God in the flesh, showing us the way to heaven! Life on earth would never be the same; it changed from the moment of His birth. He called all of us to Him as He did other ordinary people: fishermen, tentmakers, tax collectors, and homemakers.

Since Jesus ascended to heaven following the Resurrection, we still wait for Him to return as He promised. Not only at the Advent season, but also all year long, we wait, looking upward, ready to welcome God Incarnate, our *Abba*, into our hearts.

1. Have you ever had a special surprise for which you had to wait? Explain.

2. Have you ever accepted Jesus into your heart? Are you still waiting, or do you already know the wonderful miracle of a second birth inside your heart, when God comes again to earth, as His Holy Spirit fills your inner spirit with the joy and peace that passes all understanding? If you haven't experienced this miracle, simply follow the steps below.

    a. Read Romans 3:23. God is a holy God. Since all people have sinned (committed some form of evil, such as hurting others, breaking promises, or engaging in sinful behavior), your sin separates you from the holy God, who cannot tolerate the presence of evil.

b. Read Romans 6:23*a*. God is a just God. He alone is holy enough to bring perfect justice (which we want, to prevent chaos and anarchy in the world). As a just God, He punishes evil. Since you have sinned, you stand in danger of His punishment: death and eternal separation from Him.

c. Read Romans 6:23*b*. God is a loving God. He alone is perfect love. Though He is holy and just, He loves you unconditionally. Because He loves you so much, He has a plan for your salvation instead of your punishment: He sent His own Son, Jesus, to die in your place. And here's the best news. His costly sacrifice costs you nothing. It's a free gift you simply accept.

3. If you want to be saved, tell God, right now. First tell Him you're sorry for your sin, meanness, and selfishness. Ask God to forgive you. Promise you'll live for Him from now on, not for evil. Then welcome Him into your heart, to help you live for Him daily. Rejoice that you are born again!

———◆◆◆◆◆◆◆◆◆◆———

Making His Decision

BY JOY CLARY BROWN

Arise, shine; for your light has come! And the glory of the Lord is risen upon you.
—Isaiah 60:1 (NKJV)

After the birth of our first daughter, Friday afternoon became my "outing" for the week. On that afternoon, my husband kept our baby while I volunteered as a tutor at the school for teenagers with cerebral palsy. The students became such an important part of my life, I found it impossible to limit my concern for them to my few hours of teaching on Friday afternoons.

For months, Raleigh, North Carolina, had been buzzing with excitement over the upcoming Billy Graham Crusade. My husband and I were actively involved in preparing for it.

I asked the students at the school if any of them would like to go to the crusade. Three students eagerly accepted my invitation: Rodney, Skip, and Shirley. After receiving the appropriate permission from their guardians, I made arrangements to transport the students. Two special friends, Pat and John, had created a wonderful vehicle before the days of minivans; they purchased an old cab and removed one of two backseats that faced each other, leaving a floor space large enough to accommodate the students and their crutches.

The big night arrived. The students seemed as excited as we were when my husband and I picked them up from their homes. We arrived at Carter Stadium where the crusade was being held and worked our way through the throngs of people.

I was helping to interpret for the deaf during the services, so our seats were in the third level of the stadium, directly across the field from the podium. This arrangement allowed the deaf attendees to look past the interpreters over to Billy Graham and the other participants.

The service was everything I dreamed it would be and more. The music was uplifting, the testimonies were inspiring, and the message was powerful. I felt as though the air were electric with the presence of the Holy Spirit.

As the message was concluding, a challenging invitation was extended. I watched as counselors began making their way down the stairs to the field. Then a question struck me: did my students feel led to respond to the invitation? I was so caught up in what was happening, I had failed to consider that possibility.

I leaned over to them and whispered, "If any of you feels God speaking to your heart and you want to go forward, just let me know."

All three immediately began reaching for their crutches. I could hardly believe my eyes! Knowing that we had three flights of stairs to descend, I feared they would not be able to get across the field before the invitation ended. "Would you like for me to get some ushers to help carry you down?"

They each politely refused my offer, explaining, "This is something we want to do on our own." Laboriously they made their way down, step after step. We had only reached the top of the final flight of stairs when I heard the invitation concluding. Once again, I extended the offer for assistance, and realizing that they might miss this opportunity, they agreed.

The ushers carried the first two students down the steps and onto the field, where they quickly made their way across the stadium grounds. I was walking with the last student, Rodney.

As we reached ground level, Rodney moved forward as fast as his feet and crutches would allow him. Billy Graham began leading those who had come forward in the sinner's prayer. Walking beside Rodney, I heard him say aloud, *Father, forgive me for I am a sinner.* For a moment I paused and glanced up at the third level, and how far he had come to make his decision. Then I turned back and continued walking with him as I heard him ask Jesus to come into his heart!

Needless to say, the ride home was a memorable one. All three students were bubbling with excitement over the decisions they had made and what they had experienced.

The next morning, a close friend called and asked if I had seen the *Raleigh News and Observer.* My copy was still in the yard. She prompted me to get the paper and open it to a certain page. "There's a picture of you with a boy on crutches in the newspaper," she explained.

As I opened to that page, I saw a big picture of Rodney and me walking across the stadium field. A photographer at the crusade had taken it during the invitation. The caption of the picture read, "Making His Decision."

Studying every detail of the picture, I noticed something: a faint glow of light was on the ground, encircling Rodney. Even though I was directly beside him, I was not in the light. However, it completely surrounded Rodney's feet and crutches!

That night when I returned to the stadium for the continuation of the crusade, I curiously walked onto the field to try to look for anything that could've caused that light. Was it a discolored patch of grass on the field? Was he walking near a light post causing a reflection? What was the mysterious light that encircled this new believer? I saw nothing on or near the field that could have caused the light.

Suddenly, I knew the answer to the mystery! Somehow the anonymous photographer had caught on film the very moment Rodney opened his heart to receive Jesus Christ. The light that encircled Rodney's twisted legs was none other than the *Shekinah* glory of God.

Yes, the photographer had filmed Rodney "making his decision." And the glory of the Lord was risen upon him!

⤟⤟⤟ MEDITATION MOMENTS ⤟⤟⤟

1. Have you experienced a life-changing encounter with Jesus Christ?

2. Are you daily walking in His light?

When You Are Not the Miracle

BY CHERIE NETTLES

Indeed, he who watches over Israel will neither slumber nor sleep.
—Psalm 121:4 (NIV)

At age 19, I was obviously the youngest person in the rheumatologist's or arthritis/autoimmune doctor's waiting area, which was evidence of the untimeliness of the disease's attack on my body. As I scanned the room, I saw many people upon whom the disease had taken a terrible toll. One woman in particular caught my eye. I'd heard her say she had "rheumatoid." Despite severe crippling, she hummed a joyful song.

I stole another look. What I saw took my breath away and filled my eyes with tears. Her hands were deformed and drawn up, yet she held her knitting needle tightly and hummed "Amazing Grace" in a manner that everyone knew she believed its message. I lowered my head as tears streamed down my face. "Rheumatoid." That's the kind of arthritis I had.

God, please no, I prayed, *I can't do this. My hands, God, please don't let this disease do that to my hands! What about my wedding day? I want my hands to be pretty when my husband slips on my wedding band.* I was attending college for an "MRS" degree, and marriage was on the forefront of my mind.

I was called from the waiting room to see the doctor, and I never saw that woman again, but her humming continued to ring in my ears. The joy that radiated from her tune had pierced my heart as she had praised God in the midst of her suffering.

With a tear-stained face, I asked my doctor if the crippling effects also would attack my hands. (It had already attacked my feet and knees.) He told me rheumatoid arthritis almost always started in the knees and the hands, and since I'd already had one knee surgery, the likelihood of my hands being affected was almost definite. I left his office still in tears, praying, *God, please protect my hands. I can handle this disease anywhere, but not in my hands.*

Years later, Mike and I met. We knew God meant us to be together and set a date for the wedding. I continued to worry how the arthritis might flare and inflame and contort my fingers.

Shortly before my wedding day, my arthritic pain began to subside. On April 22, 1989, I walked down the aisle into the arms of Mike, my knight in shining armor (actually in a black tuxedo). He slipped my wedding band onto straight fingers with no arthritic damage; within two months, I was taken off all my medications. God had been faithful.

My doctor had said I needed to be off all high-risk medications for at least a year before trying to become pregnant. I didn't give his advice much thought because I had no intention of becoming pregnant. I was simply too giddy in love to think about having babies—until the early pregnancy test turned pink. On February 12, 1991, I gave birth to Alex, our son. Two years later, I gave birth to our daughter, Ashleigh. Both babies were perfectly healthy, and my disease remained in remission throughout that time.

When Ashleigh was two, I began to feel a sharp pain in my right foot. I tried to ignore the pain, but I knew deep in my heart my arthritis was flaring, and this time it was with a vengeance. Within four weeks, Mike had to physically lift me out of the bed. I started on crutches and eventually needed a wheelchair.

One night as I was rocking Ashleigh to sleep, Mike came into the room and saw me crying. He asked what was wrong, and as I answered him, my tears were spilling onto Ashleigh's beautiful face. I was scared that this time my arthritis would cripple my hands, and my desire was no longer to have pretty hands, but to be able to always hold my babies. (Our children are our babies forever!) Mike took Ashleigh and helped me into bed, and I cried myself to sleep, once again begging God to spare my hands.

Within two years, the high-risk medications began to stabilize my disease. Then one day I had a doctor's appointment to discuss a new drug being released for rheumatoid arthritis. One of the new claims was that the medication could stop the progression of the disease. My doctor wanted me to try this drug, and he wanted to begin by taking x-rays of a place on my body not attacked by the disease in order to measure the success of the new medication. The problem was finding that place, because the disease had attacked me from my eyes down to my toes. Simultaneously we said, "Hands!" My doctor wrote the order, and I took off for the x-ray department.

The next day I noticed a flash on my answering machine. It was the x-ray technician from my rheumatologist's office. She said, "Cherie, I have some good news for you; no, some great news. The doctor just read your x-rays, and he told me to call you and tell you there is absolutely no arthritic damage in your hands." I immediately began to thank God for protecting my hands from this disabling disease. His grace is amazing! And for these hands of mine—they may not be the prettiest, but for me they'll do just fine. And finally, I guess I really *am* the miracle!

God had brought me to this stage of life, and Jesus had carried my worry about my hands and having children. His yoke is easy and He makes our burdens light. We can trust that our God is always at work—He never sleeps nor does He slumber (Psalm 121:4).

—•••• MEDITATION MOMENTS ••••—

1. Are you struggling in life's circumstances? Create a timeline of your life, and mark evidence of God's faithfulness along the way. I think you'll see—you, too, are the miracle!

2. What has God taught you through the miracle stories in this book?

The Women by Design team members hope you will

look for miracles from God each day,

approach the future with faith, and

reach out to others, sharing your miracle stories

as you recognize His blessings in the ordinary moments of life.

WOMEN *by* DESIGN, a Ministry

WOMEN *by* DESIGN is a Christian ministry whose purpose is to point women to the truths of God's Holy Word, the Bible, that they may accept Jesus as their personal Savior and grow in all knowledge and truth of who they are in Christ. The WOMEN *by* DESIGN presentation style is unique, incorporating drama, music, comedy, and other forms of communication in addition to offering individual messages of inspiration. Visit the Web site at www.womenbydesign.org.

For further information about WOMEN *by* DESIGN MINISTRIES or to design a conference for your church or organization, contact:

WOMEN *by* DESIGN MINISTRIES
P. O. Box 2201
Lancaster, SC 29721-2201
(803) 285-3249
Ksowell@comporium.net

How to Use This Book

Designed as a flexible resource, this book can be used in a variety of ways:

- **Individual personal devotional:** Daily reading brings inspiration as well as a fresh look at the boundless ways of God.
- **Women's Bible study:** Let the devotions be the focus for women's Bible study sessions in your home or at church. Use the meditation moments at the end of each day's story to initiate group discussion.
- **Two-by-two devotional:** Share daily devotions with someone who is not a Christian, and lead her, one-on-one, closer to Jesus. Also enjoy these devotions with a Christian friend, pondering together, in unstructured format, the goodness of God, as demonstrated in these true stories of inspiration.

WOMEN *by* DESIGN MINISTRIES, INC.

New Hope® Publishers is a division of WMU®,
an international organization that challenges Christian believers
to understand and be radically involved in God's mission.
For more information about WMU, go to www.wmu.com.
More information about New Hope books may be found
at www.newhopepublishers.com. New Hope books
may be purchased at your local bookstore.

Books to Study
TOGETHER

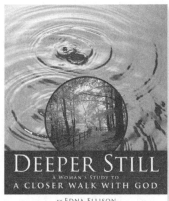

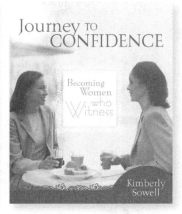

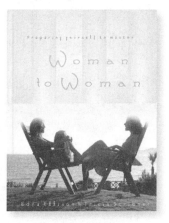

Deeper Still
*A Woman's Study
to a Closer Walk with God*
Edna Ellison
ISBN-10: 1-59669-013-5
ISBN-13: 978-1-59669-013-4

Journey to Confidence
Becoming Women Who Witness
Kimberly Sowell
ISBN-10: 1-56309-923-3
ISBN-13: 978-1-56309-923-6

Woman to Woman
Preparing Yourself to Mentor
Edna Ellison and Tricia Scribner
ISBN-10: 1-56309-949-7
ISBN-13: 978-1-56309-949-6

Available in bookstores everywhere

NEW HOPE
P U B L I S H E R S

For information about these books or any New Hope® product, visit www.newhopepublishers.com.